LEADING
POSITIVE
SAFETY

WHY 86% OF SAFETY CULTURES ARE NEGATIVE,
AND HOW YOURS DOESN'T HAVE TO BE.

DR VANESSA COOK AND ANTHONY GIBBS

We welcome you to join our Positive
Safety Community to upskill with free
learning resources and engage other
likeminded safety professionals.

Published by Vivid Publishing
A division of Fontaine Publishing Group
P.O. Box 948, Fremantle
Western Australia 6959
www.vividpublishing.com.au

A catalogue record for this
book is available from the
National Library of Australia

ACKNOWLEDGEMENTS

As we reflect on the completion of *Leading Positive Safety*, we are deeply grateful to the individuals and organisations whose unwavering support and contributions have brought this project to fruition. Their dedication to promoting positive safety practices has significantly enriched the content of this book.

First and foremost, we extend our heartfelt gratitude to the esteemed book contributors who graciously shared their insights, experiences, and compelling stories. Craig Wise of Queensland Alumina Limited; David Savio of Lifeblood; Robyn Heap of Lawson Grains; Linda Murry of Hay Point; David Pope of Pope HSE; Kenan Hibberd of Unitywater; Dr Kirstine Hulse of NZ Product Accelerator; Rod Maule of Australia Post; Anthony Butcher of Synlait Milk Ltd; Benny Mathews of Kmart & Target Group; Warren Smith of Incident Analytics – your invaluable contributions have added depth and authenticity to our exploration of positive safety. Our sincerest thanks for your openness and candour.

A special acknowledgment goes to the Sentis team, whose dedication and collaboration have been instrumental throughout this journey. David Brewster, our brilliant writing partner, played a pivotal role in shaping the narrative. Dr Amy Hawkes and the research team provided rigorous analysis, while Ben Carnell, Thibault Vincent, and the Client Solutions Team offered crucial insights into client issues and context. Our gratitude extends to Eagan Barnett, Belinda Mathie, and the HUB team for their continuous feedback and support. Chief Strategy Officer Alex Fernando ensured a focus on metrics and critical risk, and Corinne Wong and Sarah

Allan from the marketing team provided valuable input on the book's title, graphic elements, and promotion. Shannon Roberts Gibbs, your expertise in psychosocial safety has been invaluable, and we appreciate your guidance. To the entire Sentis team, thank you for being our unwavering cheer squad.

To the client organisations and safety leaders with whom we've had the privilege of working, your ongoing support for Sentis has been the bedrock of our inspiration. Understanding your challenges, people, and goals has fuelled our commitment to promoting positive safety practices. This book is a testament to the collaborative journey we've shared, and we extend our gratitude for your trust and partnership.

A heartfelt thank you is due to our key collaborators who played pivotal roles in ensuring the professional presentation and printing of this book. Karen Crombie of Exact Editing, Frank Winters of Six String Design, Jason Swiney of Fontaine Publishing Group Australia, proof-reader Gayle Oddy, and Mark Gibbs, fondly known as Ant's dad, who provided invaluable insights during the review process – your contributions have elevated the quality of our work.

Finally, a special acknowledgment goes to Tony O'Brien, Managing Director of Sentis and founder of Banyula Conservation Reserve. Your visionary leadership has been a driving force behind Sentis, inspiring us to make a positive impact on the safety leaders, organisations, and communities we interact with. Your wholehearted support for this book empowers us to fulfil our mission and create a groundswell of organisations leading positive safety. Thank you for your unwavering commitment to excellence and positive change.

With deepest gratitude,
Anthony Gibbs and Dr Vanessa Cook

CONTENTS

EXECUTIVE SUMMARY

The landscape of safety is changing. Of course, this has been true throughout history.

More than 100 years ago, the industrial revolution reshaped society as we transitioned towards more efficient and stable manufacturing processes globally. As well as the benefits, however, it also brought horrendous working conditions in factories and mines that were dangerous and unforgiving places for the men, women and children who worked there.

During this time people banded together and formed unions, demanding better working conditions and protection from an economic climate in which company owners were under no regulatory obligation and had no financial accountability to provide a safe environment for their workers. This was the start of workplace safety as we know it.

The concept of workplace wellness then started to evolve with the emergence of Employee Assistance Programs (EAPs) in the 1950s, and then broader health and wellbeing programs appeared, spurred on by various occupational health and safety movements in the 1970s. During this period, worksite wellness was motivated primarily by cost containment.[1]

The focus on worker wellbeing slowly gained momentum over time with the growth in literature on stress and wellbeing (occupational health) through the '90s, albeit as a separate and somewhat lower priority than

---

1 Reardon, J. (1998). The history and impact of worksite wellness. *Nursing Economics*, 16(3), 117–121.

physical safety. Then in 2017, the #MeToo social movement heightened awareness of the prevalence of harassment at work, and this went on to highlight the importance of inclusion and diversity and draw attention to broader workplace culture issues.

If the history of workplace safety were read as a story, the real plot twist came in the form of, dare we say it, the unprecedented global COVID pandemic. The pandemic swiftly shut down all but essential services worldwide. Organisations everywhere had to quickly acclimatise to remote work, and leaders had the daunting responsibility of managing the physical and mental wellbeing of their teams remotely.

By the end of 2022, people everywhere were all 'pivoted' out. The pandemic and the fear, uncertainty, and disconnection that it brought had challenged our accepted frames around what was 'normal' and changed our expectations of work. Meanwhile, ISO 45003 was introduced in June 2021, providing the first global standard for organisations on how to manage psychosocial risks in order to build safer and healthier workplaces.

In this post-pandemic world, physical and psychological health and safety can no longer be disjointed compliance activities managed concurrently but separately by the HSE and HR teams. The old paradigms around safety no longer stack up in the modern safety context. Despite the significant reduction in workplace injuries and incidents over the last 40 years, what we know from our extensive research is that 86% of organisations are operating with a *negative safety culture*, which is entirely or almost entirely reliant on compliance.

Safety has historically been driven by fear – fear of punishment, fear of job or incentive loss, and fear of social vilification. From the perspective of our brains, this evokes a threat reaction. Don't get caught; don't report and for goodness' sake; don't upset the apple cart. No wonder most organisations are stuck in a compliance culture, where workers carry out mandated safety requirements, especially (or only) when they know someone is looking, but dare to give no more.

Now is the time to move from a reactive, legislation-driven, conventional safety approach to a proactive, values-driven, positive safety approach. We are leaning into this need by leading a shift from viewing safety as simply harm reduction or the absence of injury, to seeing safety as a positive force that can significantly improve the quality of life for individuals and, consequently, drive greater efficiency and operational success for organisations.

Instead of focusing on the absence of harm or a reduction in incident rates, organisations can create a culture where a sense of clarity, confidence, and collaboration exists; a culture where workers support one another in a trusting and psychologically safe environment to learn and improve the way work is done. This shift supports the integration of psychological health into the safety mindset and focuses on building a workplace safety culture that enables people to thrive and bring their best selves to work.

The positive safety approach takes a holistic view of safety in which the physical, social, and psychological experiences of the worker are understood. When looking at safety as the interaction between these three experiences, it becomes clear why traditional safety initiatives have had limited success. For example, investing heavily in improving the physical work environment does little to improve safety performance in a cultural context of unsupportive leadership, workforce disengagement, and a perceived lack of leadership commitment to the workers' wellbeing and safety experience.

Investing in all three dimensions of safety experience enables workers to feel safe, well, and engaged. This in turn leads to reduced injuries: (e.g., Christian etc al[2]) and reduced absenteeism and turnover, as well as increased engagement and job satisfaction. Safety is fuelled by a greater, more autonomous, and integrated source of motivation.

Our research shows a significant correlation between all three experiences of safety and safety citizenship behaviours. Workers want to go beyond

---

2 Christian, M. S., Bradley, J. C., Wallace, J. C., & Burke, M. J. (2009). Workplace Safety: A Meta-analysis of the roles of person and situation factors.Journal of Applied Psychology, 94(5), 1103-1127.

minimum expectations and demonstrate discretionary safety behaviours, assisting others to perform their work safely, speaking up about safety concerns, and volunteering suggestions to change the way work is done to make it safer.

This is not a pie-in-the-sky dream of safety utopia, but the reliable and attainable outcomes that can be attained when positive safety is properly implemented. Drawn from over 100 Safety Climate Survey items, our research indicates that four of the top five strengths identified by employees are found in the social experience of safety. The positive trends identified relate to strong feelings of support for safety within the team as well as a strong connection with supervisors. Top performing organisations are more likely to have a blame-free learning approach to incident investigations, more likely to have senior leaders spending time out in the field building relationships and demonstrating curiosity and active care, and more likely to be enjoying a positive psychological safety climate.

The top areas of opportunity for organisations also relate to the social experience of safety. Interestingly, however, they do not relate to the social support provided by the immediate team and supervisor. Instead, they relate to activities at the organisational or leadership level, such as the management of mistakes, consideration of employees' input in decision making, the recognition of safe behaviour and the communication of change.

This book is based on our 20-plus years of research and client engagement. We have also consulted deeply with industry, including with clients who have demonstrated success in implementing positive safety and with experts outside our own company. We bring these together later in the book when outlining and demonstrating our eight principles of positive safety.

We then offer a playbook that outlines the key jobs to be done in order to progress your positive safety journey: jobs at the board and CEO level, at the senior leader level and at the frontline leader level. The eight principles are brought to life by stories from some of our clients who share their lived experiences and wisdom.

This playbook will enable you to attract and retain good employees who expect more than going home unharmed; they are looking for a positive and engaging workplace culture that adds value and is beneficial to their wellbeing. It will also enable you to uplift the capability and capacity of your leadership to create teams that are diverse, inclusive, and supportive, and that can influence increased engagement, wellbeing, job satisfaction, performance, and safety outcomes.

The landscape of safety has changed. It is no longer just about reducing incidents with rules, regulations, and PPE. It's about having the courage and conviction to set the conditions for optimal safety, where employees, teams, and organisations thrive.

It's about making safety positive.

1.

HOW SERIOUS ARE WE ABOUT SAFETY, REALLY?

*"With integrity, you have nothing to fear,
since you have nothing to hide.*

*With integrity, you will do the right thing,
so you will have no guilt."*

~ Zig Ziglar

"Safety is our number one priority," was something Stockton Rush said a lot. The founder and CEO of submersible company OceanGate took an unorthodox approach to the design of the company's underwater vehicles. As a result, the safety of their vehicles often came up in interviews.

"Safety is our number one priority," Rush wrote in a 2018 press release announcing the launch of *Titan*, a submersible designed to explore the wreck of the *Titanic*. *"We believe real-time health monitoring should be standard safety equipment on all manned submersibles."*

Titan's real-time monitoring system was designed to check the condition of its hull during deep dives, when it would be subjected to extremely high pressures. With nine acoustic sensors and 18 strain gauges, the monitoring system would keep tabs on the cylindrical carbon-fibre hull and its interface with the titanium domes on each end. The intention was that the sensors would give the pilot sufficient advance warning of a potential problem to allow a safe return to the surface before a catastrophic failure.

The problem was that the safety system Rush was describing was, in fact, no safety system at all. Yes, the analysis that his system conducted would detect when a component was about to fail – it was designed to do that during hull testing as part of the design process. What it *wasn't* designed to do was provide operational feedback, because, in practice, the time between a warning and failure of the hull was highly likely to be far too short to allow resurfacing in time.

Nevertheless, Rush, who preferred to label the cutting of corners as *innovation*, had made the decision to sidestep the independent testing usually imposed on new submersible designs. This was despite the fact that *Titan* used materials and a design philosophy that were quite different from any previous submersible used to dive four kilometres deep. Rush managed to spin the fact that his sub required a hull warning system to sound like it was safer and more advanced than others, when clearly the opposite was true.

Ironically, it would seem that "*Safety is our number one priority*" were Stockton Rush's famous last words. In June 2023, the world learnt that *Titan* had very likely suffered a violent and cataclysmic implosion that killed Rush and his four passengers in milliseconds.

In the aftermath of the tragedy, evidence of behaviours in stark contrast to Rush's verbalised commitment to safety would come to light. Rush had been incredibly strategic in ensuring he was legally protected, by operating outside US jurisdiction. He had intentionally ignored industry standards – and the laws of physics – in the name of minimising costs masquerading as innovation. In one almost comic example, OceanGate had apparently used a Sony PlayStation 3 controller to operate the submersible. Rush had allegedly disregarded advice and fired people, including experts in the field of submersibles, who had raised or reported safety concerns.

Other favourite sayings of Rush came to light after the much-publicised loss of *Titan*, which highlight attitudes very much at odds with the "*Safety is our number one priority*" mantra. These include such comments as, "*If you're not breaking things, you're not innovating*," and that he'd "*grown tired of industry players who try to use a safety argument to stop innovation*," and the particularly horrifying, "*We have heard the baseless cries of 'You are going to kill someone!' way too often.*"

The tale of Stockton Rush, OceanGate and the *Titan* is a particularly grim example of how proclaiming safety as the top priority and enacting that commitment can be two entirely different things.

Similar discrepancies between a publicly voiced commitment to safety and the demonstrated behaviours, actions, and decisions have underscored many disasters throughout history.

Few will forget the harrowing images of the tsunami that swept across the Japanese region of Tōhoku and the city of Sendai following a massive earthquake on March 11, 2011. The disaster triggered subsequent serious damage to the Fukushima Daiichi Nuclear Power Plant, including core meltdowns and the release of a large amount of radioactive material into the environment.

An independent investigation report found that the causes of the Daiichi accident had been foreseeable and that the plant operator, Tokyo Electric Power Company (TEPCO), had failed to meet basic safety requirements such as risk assessment, preparing for containing collateral damage, and the development of evacuation plans. The company admitted that they could have taken steps to prevent a catastrophic accident by adopting more extensive safety measures.

The investigation also discovered years of collusion between TEPCO, industry regulators, and politicians and that senior leaders had actively hidden safety concerns. The company dismissed the possibility of it being hit by a massive tsunami, even though they could not produce supporting data. There had also been no safety improvements to the Fukushima Daiichi plant since 2002.

Ultimately, at the heart of this disaster was the influence of leaders in positions of power, combined with a culture that does not empower people to speak up. The chair of the investigation, Kiyoshi Kurokawa, wrote: "*Its fundamental causes are to be found in the ingrained conventions of Japanese culture: our reflexive obedience, our reluctance to question authority, our devotion to 'sticking with the program', our groupism, and our insularity… This conceit was reinforced by the collective mindset of Japanese bureaucracy, by which the first duty of any individual bureaucrat is to defend the interests of his organisation. Carried to an extreme, this led bureaucrats to put organisational interests ahead of their paramount duty to protect public safety.*"[2]

The Fukushima accident was a profoundly humanmade disaster – and while Japanese culture may have played a part, it was by no means the sole cause. Any culture in which challenge is unwelcome and people capitulate to the will of higher powers would have had the same outcome. This accident could and should have been foreseen and prevented.

A similar, if less explosive, story plays out in any number of workplaces in Australia and beyond. Enter almost any industrial site – mining, manufacturing, construction, and so on – and a commitment to safety appears to be everywhere. Even before passing through the gate, you'll likely see the literal signs of a strong safety focus, such as billboards with safety messages and an electronic counter displaying the tally of injury-free days.

For anyone working on site, there are safety briefings, safety equipment,

---

2 The official report of Fukushima Nuclear Accident Independent Investigation Commission. https://www.nirs.org/wp-content/uploads/fukushima/naiic_report.pdf

risk assessments, and safe operating procedures. There are the posters and targets, the espoused values and the slogans, the regulations, and the incentives. Metrics of safety performance are tied to individual performance, perhaps including remuneration. In short, safety is everywhere, and the casual visitor would be right to believe that this equates to a genuine commitment to safety from the company.

But does it?

The reality is that around the world, hundreds of people lose their lives at work every year, and thousands are injured. This is no surprise to many workers whose felt experience of safety is very different to that espoused by their leaders. As we will unpack in more detail, many workers live with a sense that their leaders' real priority is making money. *"They don't care about us; they don't care about safety. They care about production"*[3] is a sentiment that comes through all too often in our own research.

This needs to change. If companies are serious about safety, then they must address the gap between what they say and what they do. The term 'companies', of course, speaks to leadership. Addressing the safety attitudes and behaviours of employees and individual contributors is important, certainly. But leaders need to take responsibility for the powerful influence that their decisions and behaviours, and the felt safety climate, have on those they lead.

Unequivocally, this can be done. A less well-known story that came out of the Tōhoku disaster is that of another nuclear power plant, at Onagawa, 100 kilometres north across Sendai Bay from the Fukushima plant.

Operated by the Tōhoku Electric Power Company, the Onagawa facility was 60 kilometres closer to the epicentre of the earthquake than its counterpart, and it shared similar disaster conditions. Yet its three operating reactors

---

3 Access the Driving a Positive Safety Culture report 2020 from the List of Resources at the end of the book.

were shut down successfully and safely, and the plant remained remarkably undamaged.

The fundamental difference between the two cases boils down to leadership and their genuine prioritisation of safety. One difference between the two nuclear sites was that Onagawa's reactor buildings sit at a higher elevation than the Fukushima reactor buildings. This was not a coincidence or good luck.

Before beginning construction in 1980, Tōhoku Electric conducted surveys and simulations aimed at predicting potential tsunami levels, using local and worldwide data. Their initial predictions showed that tsunamis in the region historically had an average height of about three metres. Based on that, the company constructed its plant at 14.7 metres above sea level, well in excess of past inundation levels. In doing so, they were planning for the unprecedented. When the unprecedented happened, as it did in March 2011, the plant's safety systems functioned as designed: the reactors automatically shut down without damage.[4]

By comparison, the decision makers at the TEPCO plant had prioritised cost minimisation when the construction started in 1969. They removed 25 metres from the 35-metre natural seawall in front of the Daiichi plant and built the reactors only 10 metres above sea level.

Perhaps the most important difference between the two plants lay in their attitudes toward safety, starting from senior management and cascading down through every level. At the Onagawa plant, the persistent attitude was that safety was a valued and respected priority in its own right, independent of cost and profitability. This attitude drove the behaviours of employees and management, and subsequently created an environment in which the plant was properly prepared for disaster.

---

4 Ryu, A & Meshkati, N. (2014). Onagawa: The Japanese nuclear power plant that didn't melt down on 3/11. https://thebulletin.org/2014/03/onagawa-the-japanese-nuclear-power-plant-that-didnt-melt-down-on-3-11/

At the Fukushima plant, the prevailing theme seemed to be that safety was only important as long as it could be achieved within budget, leading to a general attitude that near enough was good enough. As they ultimately learnt the hard way, it wasn't.

Researchers who investigated the contrasting outcomes at the Onagawa and Fukushima plants noted how organised, collaborative, and intentional the response was at the former location. Workers were well practiced with the steps they needed to take if a tsunami approached. Importantly, the researchers attributed this situation to the attitudes of senior leaders in the company, who were adamant about safety protocols and advocated forcefully for safety, and so influenced a strong safety culture in which spoken commitment matched actual practice.

The impact of this excellent leadership reached further than just the workers at the plant. Following the tsunami, 200 to 300 residents of the town of Onagawa took refuge in the nuclear plant's gymnasium. The plant provided a safe haven for the locals, in stark contrast to the Fukushima plant. The damage to that facility forced the evacuation of thousands from their homes, many of whom will likely never return.

So, how serious about safety are we? We firstly recognise that no leaders want people to be hurt in the line of duty – no matter how senior and removed from the 'coalface' of the work, no matter how responsible for the financial success of a company. We also recognise the difficulty of acknowledging and closing the gap between safety as talked and safety as walked. It takes a certain boldness, *chutzpah*, audacity even, to be a disruptor and dare to do things differently. But this is exactly what we desperately need.

If you want to be a true instrument of change and have the courage and conviction to lead a positive safety culture, read on.

2.

THE CURRENT STATE OF SAFETY

"If the brutal facts are not faced by leaders,
the brutal reality sets in."

~ Andy Grove

Many of us experience modern safety practices on a daily basis. In road safety, for instance, today's cars are immensely safer than their earlier counterparts. At the same time, more and more safety features are being incorporated into our major roads.

Millions of dollars have been spent installing wire rope barriers on motorways to prevent cars from straying into oncoming traffic or into trees along the roadside. Rumble strips are also standard on many regional roads as a warning to fatigued or distracted drivers who drift out of their lanes. In our major cities, even the smallest road or building works are supported by traffic management teams, well stocked with cones, signs and stop/go signals.

All of this is complemented, of course, by measures to ensure compliance – the policing of speed limits, seatbelt wearing, mobile phone use, running of red lights and so on, with larger and larger fines imposed on those caught breaking the rules. The focus on safety in many areas of our lives has accelerated over the last 20 years or so as the financial and human cost of injuries and fatalities is increasingly recognised by governments, corporations, and society at large.

The same applies in workplaces.

Meet Travis, an apprentice fitter whose employer specialises in large industrial projects. His current job involves working with a team in the field on the construction of a pipeline. By the time Trav picks up his tools each day and heads out to the work site, he's covered from head to foot in company-supplied personal protective equipment (PPE): hard-hat, safety goggles, earplugs, hi-vis long-sleeved shirt, work gloves, long work pants, kneepads, steel-toed boots – the works.

Before starting on the site for the first day, he was given a safety induction that included a briefing on safety procedures specific to the site, including processes for reporting a hazard, a near miss, or any injury to himself or someone he is working with. Each day before they go out, the team and their supervisor have a 'pre-start' meeting to plan for the day and raise any issues – including safety concerns – from the previous day.

As they head out, every piece of electrical equipment they are carrying has been tested and tagged as safe to use. Ladders, harnesses, and any other access gear they might need has undergone similar checks.

The Occupational Health and Safety officer for the job is hard-nosed about compliance, effectively a police officer on the beat, alert, and hunting for anyone failing to wear their PPE properly or not adhering to a procedure. Anyone who cuts corners is at risk of being thrown off the site and potentially banned from it altogether.

On top of all that, Travis knows that if he is injured, a well-developed worker's compensation scheme will provide both financial support and rehabilitation to help him recover and return to work as quickly (and safely) as possible. He also knows that, ultimately, he has the protection of state and federal laws, should his employer fail to provide a 'safe workplace'. It's a lot, but none of it is unusual to Travis or to anyone else on the job. It's all standard practice and has been for some time. Anything less would feel, well, weird.

That's what safety *looks* like in 2024.

But what is the real life *experience* of workplace safety for people like Travis? Does all this gear, the safety procedures and the policing of compliance make them *feel* safe, well, and engaged as they go about their work? Our research indicates that for a large majority of workers, there is a wide gap between the visible face of safety in their organisations and the felt experience of the *individuals* within those organisations.

The truth about safety culture and climate

Over recent years, we have conducted wide-ranging research into the state of safety culture and safety climate. In our *Driving a Positive Safety Culture* report (2020),[5] the research was based on our safety culture and climate diagnostic, which is a combination of our Onsite Safety Evaluation (qualitative data gathered through interviews and focus groups) and the Safety Climate Survey (a quantitative questionnaire). The study included 73 sites, across eight industries, in nine countries.

We conducted over 5,000 face-to-face interviews and 562 focus groups, and over 20,000 individuals participated in the Safety Climate Survey. The combination of research methods in our diagnostic approach ensured that the quantitative strength of our Safety Climate Survey data was complemented by the qualitative richness of interviews from our Onsite Safety Evaluation assessment.

5 Access the Driving a Positive Safety Culture report 2020 from the List of Resources at the end of the book.

Distinguishing safety culture and safety climate

In our work, we make a clear distinction between the concept of 'safety culture' and that of 'safety climate'.

Safety culture is an organisation's shared attitudes, beliefs, and values about safety. Essentially, it's 'the way things are done around here'. Safety culture influences safety performance and is a significant factor in predicting the likelihood of safety incidents. But it isn't easily observed. Safety culture is deeply embedded into the fabric of an organisation, often below conscious awareness. To assess safety culture we use qualitative research including focus groups, interviews, and observations.

Safety climate reflects employees' shared perceptions of the extent to which safety is valued within an organisation. Safety climate can be considered a snapshot of an organisation's safety culture at any point in time. It can give insight into employees' perceptions of the physical, social, and psychological experiences of safety. Safety climate is more easily measured quantitatively than safety culture, and for this we use survey tools such as our Safety Climate Survey.[6]

Safe Work Australia makes a useful distinction between safety culture and safety climate. It describes safety culture as akin to an organisation's personality, whereas safety climate is more like its emotions. Like someone's personality, the safety culture is fairly well embedded, changing little over time. The safety climate, like someone's emotions, can be more volatile as the 'mood' of the organisation changes from day to day and can be influenced by current events.

6 Interested in gaining a snapshot of your organisation's safety climate? Access a link to a free Safety Climate Self-Assessment from the List of Resources at the end of the book.

A staggering 86% of the sites surveyed in our study displayed what we would describe as *negative* and compliance-focused safety cultures. Only two sites (3%) displayed a clearly positive safety culture. Needless to say, there remains plenty of scope for improvement.

While the numbers are powerful, equally impactful are the stories we heard from some of our diagnostic participants. The following quotes represent a small sample.

> *"If you report something then you have an issue. It's a blame game."*

> *"A guy broke his arm while adjusting a bucket on a dozer with the operator still in it. Both were fired 12 hours later, but we didn't record the injury."*

> *"'I wouldn't bother trying to report [an incident] again. My experience was so poor. Why bother? It just disappears into cyberspace."*

> *"Safety culture is largely focused on the correct paperwork, not necessarily doing the job right."*

These, and many similar negative comments, point to safety cultures in which the numbers matter more than the wellbeing of the individuals involved – where protecting leadership and the company from the consequences of safety breaches is considered more important than the protection of workers' welfare. The attitude is that 'recording zero' is the priority, regardless of the reality on the frontline, or at least, this is what people perceive that their leaders expect. This creates behaviours that are about avoiding reports rather than avoiding accidents.

The root cause of the negativity reflected in these comments doesn't rest with a lack of PPE, training, or data. The problem goes deeper than that: it's about what's going on in people's heads and not just on the shop floor. It's about attitudes and the behaviours that come from them, starting with senior leadership and cascading down to the front line. In other words, it's about more than the conventional, equipment-and-procedures approach to safety improvement that has prevailed for many decades. It's about something that turns out to be much more complicated than those factors: people and their brains.

To reiterate: these negative safety cultures dominated our diagnostics by a large margin.

On closer analysis of the data, a clear picture emerges of the reasons why so many organisations are stuck with negative safety cultures. Here's what we found to be the most significant factors at play:

1. *Safety procedures are getting in the way of work.* Most safety procedures were introduced in response to a legal obligation or to provide guidance on safe operating parameters, or both. However, at some point we seem to have become fixated on documentation as the solution to risk management, and then overindulged in creating layers of checklists and procedures.

   This, combined with the perception that procedures are often complicated, confusing, and pushed onto workers without consultation, leads to a perception amongst the workforce that procedures serve the protection of the company rather than the people. This experience leaves the workforce disengaged, and the tick-and-flick culture grows. In essence, as the survey respondent said, "*Safety culture is largely focused on correct paperwork, not necessarily doing the right job.*"

2. *Workers don't believe their leaders are committed to safety and, therefore, their wellbeing.* It's more than a little ironic that we expect workers to demonstrate helpful safety attitudes and behaviours when cost minimisation and production targets dominate leadership communications. Or when maintenance requests or ideas for improvement fall on deaf ears because they will cost money. Or when leaders turn a blind eye to safety issues and fail to role model safe attitudes and behaviours themselves.

Interestingly, our research found that there tends to be high in-team support for safety, but lower management support for safety, indicating that teams have more confidence in having each other's backs than they do in being supported and protected by their leadership team. To quote another respondent, "*It's a good message they're saying, but it's not translating into action or changes in what's actually happening in the workplace.*"

3. *Change isn't managed well and people are uncertain about the future.* There has been a lot of change in recent years, and while there is a predictable ebb and flow of change in any organisation, factors like the COVID-19 pandemic and other natural disasters have delivered many unique challenges. The way change is managed profoundly impacts the stress and anxiety levels of workers and their general feeling of safety.

    If employees feel that change is implemented without proper communication, consideration, or support, it can erode their trust and confidence in leaders. Trust is a foundational element in any organisation; once damaged, it's challenging to rebuild. A loss of trust can lead to decreased morale, reduced employee engagement, and increased staff turnover. Poorly managed change leaves people feeling that "*They don't talk to the people on the ground. It's top-down change. We feel disheartened.*"

4. *People are unwilling to report incidents and errors.* Workers may be unwilling to report hazards, incidents and near misses for a number of reasons, including fear of losing their jobs or having marks against their names, or due to cumbersome reporting processes. This poses a significant risk to organisations. When incidents go unreported, vital information about potential hazards and vulnerabilities remains hidden.

This lack of transparency prevents organisations from understanding the true state of their safety performance and implementing corrective actions. As a result, the same or similar incidents might reoccur, potentially leading to more severe consequences in the future. While many organisations have been trying to move to a blame-free culture around reporting, this just isn't the felt experience for many workers. They feel that "*Incident reporting is designed to find fault and not areas of improvement*."

5. *There is a general lack of recognition and validation for safe behaviours.* From a brain perspective, receiving recognition and reward is important. It helps us feel valued and respected and can drive our motivation to achieve outcomes. What we need to consider closely is what we reward and what consequences that will have. Incentives or bonuses based on incident-free targets will drive people to hide injuries and underreport.

In our interviews, many workers talked of incentives and recognition being tied to production targets, but often none, or very few, incentives that encouraged safe behaviours and outcomes. Receiving praise for hitting production targets when the outcome was achieved by cutting corners, for instance, sends mixed messages. It can make people feel that leaders don't really care about their wellbeing because "*Supervisors are rewarded for production, not safety. All the incentives are production-based*."

Hitting the wall: the very real consequences of negative safety cultures

Unfortunately, the cold, hard statistics reinforce our findings that safety cultures, no matter how visible they are, are a long way from perfect.

According to Safe Work Australia, there were 130,000 serious workers' compensation claims in 2020/21, and almost 200 Australians still die in workplace accidents annually. That fatality rate is down from a peak this century of over 300 in 2007; however, the trend has been flat for over a decade, rather than improving. In some industries, the rate of workplace fatalities has fallen to low levels for periods of time, only to revert to unacceptably high levels.

In 2019, Dr Sean Brady of the Queensland Department of Natural Resources, Mines and Energy reported on a review of all fatal accidents in Queensland mines and quarries from 2000 to 2019.[7] The Brady Report shows fatalities cycling between one or two a year and four or five a year, sometimes from one year to the next. There was no sign of a consistent improvement in the rate of deaths over that period. In short, we've stalled at a level that is a long way from the ideal of zero.

These statistics are not unique to Australia. Worldwide, there are still too many people losing their lives or being left with ongoing pain, disabilities, and reduced quality of life.

While the rate of physical injury has levelled off, instances of psychological injury have been on the increase, particularly since the mid-2010s. According to insurer Allianz, workers' compensation claims relating to mental health increased by 80% between 2017 and 2020, and anecdotal evidence would suggest that they are much higher, again due to the impact of the COVID-19 pandemic.

In the state of New South Wales, psychosocial injuries are climbing 15 times faster than physical injuries. Compensation claims for mental health conditions now make up around 9% of all serious workers' compensation claims. Psychological injuries have particular significance because they

---

7 Brady, S. (2019). *Review of all fatal accidents in Queensland mines and quarries from 2000 to 2019.* Department of Natural Resources, Mines and Energy. https://documents.parliament.qld.gov.au/tableOffice/TabledPapers/2020/5620T197.pdf

tend to have longer recovery times, incur higher costs and result in more time away from work than physical injuries.

Global safety trends

Canada
1,081 workers died due to work-related causes in Canada in 2021, while there were 277,217 lost-time injuries.[8]

Great Britain
135 workers died in work-related incidents in Great Britain in 2022/23 and 565,000 reported a non-fatal injury.[10]

European Union
In 2020, there were 3,355 fatal workplace accidents and 2.7 million non-fatal accidents that resulted in at least four days of lost time.[9]

United States
In 2021, a total of 5,190 fatal work injuries occurred and 2,607,900 total recordable incidents were reported.[12]

Australia
In the 2020/21 financial year, there were 169 work-related fatalities in Australia and 130,195 serious workers' compensation claims.[13]

New Zealand
In 2022, there were 59 workplace fatalities and 34,908 injuries resulting in more than a week away from work.[11]

---

8 Association of Workers' Compensation Boards of Canada, National Work Injury/Disease Statistics Program. https://awcbc.org/en/statistics/

9 Europa, Accidents at work statistics. https://ec.europa.eu/eurostat/statistics-explained/index.php?title=Accidents_at_work_statistics#:~:text=Highlights&text=There%20were%203%20355%20fatal,compared%20with%20the%20year%20before.&text=In%202020%2C%20more%20than%20a,place%20within%20the%20construction%20sector

10 Health and Safety Executive. https://www.hse.gov.uk/statistics/causinj/index.htm

11 Worksafe. https://data.worksafe.govt.nz/graph/summary/injuries_week_away

12 US Bureau of Labor Statistics, Injuries, Illnesses and Fatalities. https://www.bls.gov/iif/#:~:text=There%20were%205%2C190%20fatal%20work,increase%20from%204%2C764%20in%202020

13 Safe Work Australia, Australian Workers Compensation Statistics https://www.safeworkaustralia.gov.au/sites/default/files/2022-12/221122_awcs_infographics.pdf

While it's likely that a good proportion of this upsurge can be attributed to increased reporting (associated with increased awareness and stronger focus from regulators) rather than an increase in occurrences, this does not take away from the seriousness of the claims. Rather, it reflects the changing societal standards we have mentioned and indicates a similar trend to when physical injury at work also became more unacceptable. We will explore this further in the next chapter.

In summary, an observable commitment to safety is all around us, in our workplaces and in our everyday lives. In workplaces this visibility is reflected in the extensive PPE, the posters, the injury scoreboards, the long lists of procedures and checklists, and the repercussions punishing anyone who fails to comply.

But this visual appearance of safety is not consistent with the lived experience of safety faced by many working people – something emphasised by our own research in which 86% of surveyed sites demonstrated negative safety cultures. This truth is reflected in the ongoing rate of injuries. We have rates of serious physical injury that are higher than they should be but are not coming down. On top of that, psychological injuries are causing additional harm with increasing frequency.

Sounds pretty grim, doesn't it? Perhaps. But we'd prefer to see it as an opportunity. We'd prefer to see the current safety environment as a challenge to be met. The opportunity is to think differently, to shift from viewing safety simply as harm reduction and the absence of injuries to seeing it as a positive force – a force that can improve the quality of life for individuals and, consequently, drive greater efficiency and operational success for organisations.

The opportunity for organisations is to shift from regarding safety management as being all about policing compliance and imposing consequences – and instead create a positive safety culture in which a sense of confidence and collaboration exists; in which workers support one another in a trusting and psychologically safe environment to learn and improve the way work is done, and in which people thrive and bring their best selves to work.

For organisations that have been involved in the world of safety for some time, they need to be willing to let go of, or at least loosen, some of their immutable truths. They need to adjust their perspective on the fundamental purpose of safety management, seeing money spent on safety as an investment, not a cost. They need to question their assumptions and readjust their approach so that new, previously unimagined ideas can find their way into their minds.

This starts with understanding how we got to this point.

3.

HOW DID WE GET TO THIS POINT?

"The difficulty lies not so much in developing new ideas
as in escaping from old ones."

~ John Maynard Keynes

In October 1930, Vincent Kelly was working on the construction of the Sydney Harbour Bridge, fixing enormous rivets to steel beams on the 'deck' that would become the roadway. By now the iconic arch was complete, towering over the harbour. It was only 18 months before the bridge would officially open.

As with every worker on the bridge project since the first sod was turned in 1923, Vincent plied his trade with no safety gear to speak of. There were no helmets, no harnesses, no hearing protection, and definitely no high-vis vests. The construction company provided gloves. That was it. Workers provided their own rubber-soled leather boots, which gave them a decent grip when climbing around the steelwork – at least when it wasn't raining.

Vincent's co-worker and best mate 'Mo' Moore was a talented high diver who would later work as a coach with Australia's Olympic diving team. He trained Vincent too, in something similar to the art of high board diving. He and Vincent made plans for what they would do, should either of them fall from the bridge. Feet first was the idea. They *"might even throw in a somersault or two if they had the chance."* As it turned out, it was Vincent who had the misfortune of having to put the plan to the test!

The precise circumstances are clouded by time, but the outcome isn't. After slipping from the wooden platform on which he was working, Vincent found himself falling 182 feet (55 metres) to the water below. In the mere seconds available to him, he twisted himself around to get his feet below his body and his hands above his head before he plunged into the water. Those on the massive structure above held their collective breaths.

And then, moments later, Vincent resurfaced. He swam to a nearby boat and was taken to hospital with no more than a few broken ribs and some nasty bruising. Remarkably, he returned to work 17 days later, where he was gifted a watch by his employers and awarded a medal celebrating his survival.

Unfortunately, there were plenty of others who were not as lucky as Vincent Kelly. Over the nine years of the project, dozens of men lost their hearing or had it severely damaged, and many more were badly injured. Sixteen lost their lives. Remarkably, only two of those deaths occurred due to falls from the arch. Five lost their lives while working on the approaches to the bridge; two were killed at Moruya, south of Sydney, where granite was quarried and shaped for the bridge's pylons.

When a death occurred, work didn't stop and there was no investigation. For anyone traumatised by having witnessed a fatality at close hand, counselling amounted to a glass of medicinal brandy. Support for the families of those lost or injured was virtually non-existent. Perhaps the men would contribute half a day's pay to cover funeral costs. There was no mention of those lost when the bridge was opened.

The rise and rise of one-dimensional safety

There isn't a lot of history of safety management prior to the 20th century for the simple reason that safety wasn't on the radar.

As the machine age and mass production took hold in the late 19th century, the priority was speed of output. Accidents – indeed, lives – were cheap. A century ago, the annual fatality rate amongst American miners was 300 for every 100,000, and this was regarded as an expected cost of doing business. Workers' rights at this time were virtually non-existent. An injured worker could sue their employer, but they had little chance of success as the law placed the burden of risk mostly on the worker themselves. In addition, workers were often paid based on their output – tons of coal or pieces made – so naturally they also saw safety as a lower priority.

A number of factors contributed to a shift that had its origins early in the 20th century. Initially, workers started voting with their feet, simply leaving jobs they felt were too dangerous. Then pressure started to mount as societal expectations shifted.

Community outcry, often in response to some major incident that claimed multiple lives, along with campaigns by unions, supportive journalists and activist workers saw governments start to take notice. The first workers' compensation laws followed, placing greater liability for worker safety on their employers. With that, the monetary cost to companies for worker injuries, and especially fatalities, skyrocketed. It rose tenfold on US railroads in the early 20th century. As they say, money talks. All of a sudden it was in the boss's interest to start putting guards on machines and requiring workers to wear hard hats.

Sometimes change came down to a single individual. During construction of the Golden Gate Bridge in San Francisco, which started only two years after the opening of the Sydney Harbour Bridge, workers wore hard hats and a safety net was slung under the floor of the bridge during the roadway construction. Both of these safety precautions were initiatives of the chief project engineer, Joseph Strauss. The net saved the lives of 19 men who otherwise would have plunged to their deaths (assuming none of them had the good fortune of Vincent Kelly!).

Health and safety legislation evolved, and technology gradually improved over the remainder of the 20th century, to the point that, at the end of the century, the fatality rate in US mines had dropped to 3% of what it was a hundred years before. In the world of our contemporary apprentice Travis, whom we met earlier, he and his family can rest assured that his chances of arriving home safely every day are definitely higher than they would have been a century ago.

Characteristic of this shift, and indeed of safety management as a whole up to this point, was that it focused on *physical* safety – on the prevention of people being physically harmed – underpinned by an emphasis on ensuring compliance with safety protocols. On this we can see a straight line between the experiences of Vincent Kelly and those of the modern apprentice Travis, even if the observable safety experiences of these two men are light years apart.

Another characteristic of the evolution of safety over this period is that it was increasingly underpinned by a philosophy that safety initiatives provided protection *from* something. Individuals needed to be protected *from* physical pain, injury, disablement, and death. Leaders needed to be protected *from* the paperwork associated with injuries and near misses, from the inconvenience of managing staff shortages or having to find light duties, sometimes from losing a safety bonus and, in the worst case, from the threat of legal liability. Organisations had to be protected *from* litigation, as well as interventions from regulators, escalating insurance premiums and reputational damage.

This focus on physical harm and a reliance on compliance to protect workers, leaders, and the company from the consequences of accidents, is what we refer to as *one-dimensional safety*.

Psychosocial safety: a second dimension

Julie (not her real name) is a single mum sharing care of her three children. She took a job as a truck driver with a mining company in Western Australia, attracted by the good pay on offer plus the promise of opportunities for career progression.

It was Julie's first exposure to the mining industry, although one of her three older brothers had worked with a different company for a few years, as had a couple of her friends, and all of them had had positive experiences. It was definitely the first time she'd driven a giant truck, but she was up for a challenge and liked the idea of doing something new.

After she started the job, and throughout her training, Julie was amazed by how comprehensive the workplace's safety environment and practices were. She'd never worked anywhere with so many warning signs or such a strong emphasis on PPE, SOP (Standard Operating Procedures), and barriers. They had more safety briefings in a week than her previous employer, a retail outlet, had ever had.

There were even things called 'critical control verifications' – she'd never come across these before – which were ongoing checks that the safety environment and practices were in place and working as planned. It seemed that everyone was good about following the rules and complying with safety procedures.

Julie's brother had warned her that mine sites could be pretty macho, and that was obvious from the start, as she found herself one of very few female truckies in her crew. In fact, she was one of very few women on the site at all, and most of those worked in the offices. So, she was ready for the occasional sexist joke and a bit of patronising behaviour from time to time.

It actually ended up being worse than she expected, with some of the men throwing gendered insults at her, clearly struggling with the idea of a woman doing what they saw as a 'man's job', and others sexually harassing her with language and inappropriate touching in ways that had been socially unacceptable for a couple of decades. Nevertheless, she felt she could tough it out. Growing up with three brothers had given her a thick skin, and most of each day was spent on her own in her truck anyway.

Within a few weeks, Julie started noticing things that concerned her. The trucks, while well maintained mechanically, were often left in a mess by their previous users. Some of the cabins had a stench of stale smoke and were left littered with cigarette butts, even though smoking was strictly banned on the site. A couple of times, pornographic magazines were left on the seat by the previous operator, who knew very well that one of the women could be using the truck next. To her it felt like a sign of contempt, a signal that some of the men had no intention of changing their unprofessional behaviours just because there were a few women around.

Then she started to notice that some of the other drivers and some of the guys in the mine itself were cutting corners with safety. Mostly it was small stuff – occasionally not wearing a hard hat or hearing protection – but there were also a couple of potentially serious near-misses, including one occasion where a truck in front of her had very nearly left the road with a full load on board. To top it all off, she witnessed her supervisor bullying members of the team, pushing them into doing extra shifts or overtime, even when they tried to explain that they couldn't for family reasons.

Eventually, after Julie found herself on the end of one of these bullying episodes, she felt she had to speak up. But first she thought she would sound out a couple of the other women and Josh, one of the guys who she'd found to be supportive. To her surprise, their message was very clear: "*Don't **ever** report anything. It'll only get you into trouble, you'll make too many enemies and you might find yourself out of a job.*" Josh told her that their supervisor was a cousin of the site manager, and that they had a history of looking out for each other.

A few days later, one of the other truckies, Baz, sprained an ankle while climbing down from his truck. His injury was bad enough that he couldn't drive, so he had no choice but to report it. Julie was there at the time. The boss blamed Baz for being clumsy but refused to submit an incident report and gave Baz a couple of days of paperwork to do as unofficial light duties.

When Julie urged Baz to report the injury, he wouldn't. *"It's a waste of time,"* he shrugged. *"Management won't do anything about it, and the truth is they don't want to know because it will make their numbers look bad."* After that, Julie couldn't help giving a cynical laugh when she drove onto the site, passing a large sign advertising that there hadn't been any lost-time injuries in the last six months.

A couple of weeks later, Julie was bullied by the supervisor again. After that, she'd had enough. She made enquiries with HR and, after a bit of digging, found that there was a policy around bullying and harassment and a procedure for formal lodging of complaints. She decided to test the process and submitted the documentation. A few days later, someone from HR came around and spoke to a number of people from the team, including the supervisor. Perhaps they were taking her seriously after all? One big positive was that they seemed to be keeping her name out of it – they were talking in general terms about 'someone' having made a complaint.

Julie's supervisor was looking at her differently now. He seemed to soften his behaviour a little after that – or perhaps it was that he avoided her more. Some posters went up reminding people that bullying wasn't on, and a few weeks later a training session was held at which they watched a couple of videos about respect in the workplace. That session was peppered with crude jokes from a number of the men who clearly didn't take it seriously.

Julie heard no more about her complaint after that, and nothing really changed. The taunts and leers she received from some of her colleagues went on. The bullying and inappropriate behaviour between team members, and even from leaders towards workers, continued. Talking to the few friends Julie made over time, it seemed they never got rid of the troublemakers. They either found a way to get rid of the person making complaints, or they'd transfer someone to another site if the issue were serious enough. The place had a bad vibe, but it seemed everyone was willing to trade their physical and mental wellbeing for a fat pay packet.

By now Julie was starting to see the harsh reality of the place. All the PPE and safety procedures were disguising a broken safety culture. Any motivation to do the right thing really came from a place of fear, of not wanting to be caught or be seen making waves. When out of sight of senior management, whether in the cabin of a truck or in the break room, there were people who knew they could get away with anything, including mental and physical abuse.

Julie realised that the safety meetings were nothing but a charade. No one was seriously interested in improving safety – they were just going through the motions, more interested in keeping the numbers down than reducing harm. All in all, the mine's workforce was disengaged, just surviving as best they could in a negative and reactive culture. And while HR had responded to her complaint of bullying and made her aware of the company's EAP service, it was clear that this sort of psychological abuse wasn't seen as a safety issue – it was an HR issue that was dealt with mostly at arm's length.

When Julie realised that the sexism, harassment, and work stress were starting to get to her, affecting her mood away from work, and that she was also getting anxious about being physically injured herself, she resigned and found another job. She knew from her friends at other mines that her experience wasn't the norm for the industry, but she found herself hesitant to continue. For the time being, she decided to forgo the better pay and returned to her previous career in retail.

From one-dimensional to two-dimensional safety

Julie's case reflects many of the issues we have been discussing to this point: an observable commitment to safety that isn't matched in reality, an underlying negative safety culture, disincentives for and discouragement of the reporting of incidents and near misses, and a disengaged workforce. Julie's story also introduces something we have not yet discussed in detail: *psychosocial* safety. It highlights the fact that safety isn't merely about controlling the physical risks in a workplace, but it's also about understanding and managing the psychosocial risks. Within the field of psychology, the term 'psychosocial' is defined as the influence of social, cultural, and environmental factors on an individual's mind or behaviour. When applied to safety, psychosocial hazards are described as the social, cultural, and environmental aspects of work that have the potential to cause physical or psychological harm.

Recognition of the importance of psychosocial health for wellbeing, along with awareness of systemic psychosocial issues, has grown over the last decade or so. Seemingly overnight, the rise of the #MeToo movement in 2017 saw a step change in understanding the impact of sexual abuse, harassment, and bullying.

More broadly, we have seen growing acceptance of mental health issues alongside physical health problems as an equally valid reason for seeking rest and rehabilitation. Highly visible in this shift have been a number of prominent sportspeople who have taken precious time out of their careers to deal with mental health challenges – something that would have been unthinkable only a few years ago.

Just as the threat of increasing costs, along with community outcry and government regulation forced companies to take seriously the risks of physical harm in the 1930s, the same is happening now when it comes to the risks of psychosocial harm. As we've seen, workers' compensation claims for mental health and other psychological injuries are on the rise. Psychosocial hazards such as high work demands, workplace harassment and bullying, remote or isolated work, low job control or poor support have been associated with risks of both psychological and physical injury, including anxiety, depression, sleep disorders, substance abuse, musculoskeletal injuries, chronic disease, fatigue-related incidents, workplace and motor vehicle incidents, and self-harm or suicidal thoughts.[14, 15]

The anticipated surge in costs associated with untreated mental health issues in the Australian workforce is predicted to reach $18.6 billion by 2025. Employers have really had no option but to take psychosocial risk seriously.

In 2021, a global standard called ISO 45003 was introduced with a specific focus on providing guidelines for the management of psychosocial risks in the workplace. In the meantime, workplace health and safety regulations in Australia and many other countries increasingly stipulate that psychosocial risks be identified and managed in the same way that physical risks are.

At the time of writing this book, many developed countries have adopted similar standards or regulations. The National Standard of Canada for Psychological Health and Safety in the Workplace was introduced in 2013, and the UK's Health and Safety Executive provides management standards for stress and mental health at work covering factors such as job demands and control, work relationships, and bullying. In several EU member states, there is now more specific legislation on psychosocial risks that clarifies employer responsibilities.

All these developments have cemented the legal and ethical duty of employers to tackle psychosocial risks head-on. However, there is a danger here – a danger that organisations approach these changes with the same reactive, compliance-driven mindset with which they have traditionally addressed risks of physical harm. We see this in organisations we've worked in, which have psychosocial strategies that are limited to 'tertiary' inter-

---

14 WHO (2010). Authored by Leka, S, & Jain, A., Health Impact of Psychosocial Hazards at Work: An Overview. Geneva: World Health Organization.

15 OECD (2012), Sick on the Job?: Myths and Realities about Mental Health and Work, Mental Health and Work, OECD Publishing, Paris, https://doi.org/10.1787/9789264124523-en.

ventions, that is, interventions that swing into motion *after* the horse has bolted, focusing, say, on rehabilitation via an EAP service, as opposed to a primary intervention that would aim to prevent the harm in the first place.

Julie's experience was typical. When she looked into it, she discovered that her employer had an existing process for the reporting of psychosocial harm or threats (a tertiary response). She was also able to lodge a complaint anonymously. The response to that complaint included the mounting of posters about bullying and a short training session on the topic. However, there was no lasting change from this.

A warning sign in Julie's case was that the process and responses around her complaint were regarded as the responsibility of the human resources (HR) department, not the health and safety team. The rationale here was presumably that environmental health and safety (EHS) managers look after 'traditional' safety (usually concerned with physical harm), while HR looks after what some call the 'soft' emotional stuff of psychological harm. This is a good example of what we call 'two-dimensional' safety, and it is not unusual.

Two-dimensional safety is very similar to one-dimensional safety, but with the addition of providing tertiary interventions to support workers affected by psychological harm, responding to incidents with reactive administrative controls. A one-dimensional approach to safety only recognises and takes accountability for physical risk in order to avoid physical injury and litigation.

A two-dimensional approach to safety is a step forward, in that psychosocial risks are also a focus; however, a holistic approach to safety is difficult when responsibility for psychosocial safety has been delegated to the HR team. Intervention efforts are still reactionary and reliant on compliance, born from a motivation to avoid the negative personal and legal consequences of psychosocial harm. With respect to psychosocial harm, the hazards are not always clearly understood and the risk not effectively managed, so management is not using the appropriate controls to mitigate them. This exactly mirrors Julie's experience.

In a two-dimensional safety approach there may be some secondary interventions: workplace-level initiatives that build awareness and improve the way workers respond to stressors, such as resilience training, wellness programs, or promotional activities (e.g. posters). Such interventions are consistent with the aim of protecting workers from harm, while also providing protection for leaders from some of the same things we see in one-dimensional safety: paperwork, threats of legal liability, etc. What we tend not to see in two-dimensional safety is the implementation of primary interventions for psychosocial risk, such as initiatives to *prevent* stress and harm by removing stressors from the environment through work redesign.

Limited focus, diminishing returns and new opportunities

A hundred years on, it's hard to look back at projects like the Sydney Harbour Bridge construction and not shake our heads in wonder. The immaturity of workplace safety at that time would be unfathomable to a modern worker in a similar situation.

In stark contrast to Vincent, the contemporary experience of Travis and millions of others like him is that safety is no longer a 'nice to have'. It is a non-negotiable, with organisations and their managements held strongly accountable for their safety performance alongside turnover, profitability and other measures.[16]

Indeed, safety performance is now measured in the same way as turnover and profitability, that is, via accounting metrics. Unsophisticated measures like 'lost time injury frequency rate' (LTIFR) and 'total recordable incident

---

16 This is not to say, of course, that these improvements have been universally applied. Many millions of people across the world still work in poor conditions with close to non-existent safety standards. This is the case in both developing economies and more advanced economies. We recognise that the focus of this book is on businesses that operate with the privilege of being able to have the safety of their workers as a high priority.

frequency rate' (TRIFR) are widely used, and milestones – *427 days since a lost time injury!* – are celebrated. In addition, the definition of 'safety' within the workplace has expanded to recognise psychological harm and psychosocial risk, in line with a similar shift in societal norms.

This advancement and expansion of workplace safety is very welcome to those of us who dedicate our careers to safety. As we discussed in the last chapter, today's incidence of workplace fatalities and injuries is immensely lower than it was a hundred years ago. We've come a long way, and that's a good thing!

On the other hand, as we also demonstrated in the last chapter, safety cultures in a majority of organisations and across many industries remain stubbornly negative. The rate of serious physical injuries in most industrialised countries has stopped improving over the last 10 to 20 years, and claims due to psychological harm are increasing.

A significant contributor to this situation is the way we tend to frame industrial or workplace safety. In his review of all fatal accidents in Queensland mines and quarries from 2000 to 2019,[17] Sean Brady identified that perhaps one of the biggest stumbling blocks to reducing the number of workplace fatalities is the way the industry and indeed the general public frame safety in the mining industry.

Everyone understands that mining is a hazardous industry, and with that understanding comes an expectation that the risk of injury is an inevitable part of the job, regardless of what preventative measures might be in place. This was demonstrated in responses to our Onsite Safety Evaluations. *"We're in a risky business, and accidents are part of what we do. That's how it is,"* and, *"It's just a matter of time,"* were common sentiments. This fatalism gets in the way of the industry taking the next step.

---

17 Brady, S. (2019). *Review of all fatal accidents in Queensland mines and quarries from 2000 to 2019.* Department of Natural Resources, Mines and Energy. https://documents.parliament.qld.gov.au/tableOffice/TabledPapers/2020/5620T197.pdf

But it need not be this way. Working in a dangerous industry doesn't fundamentally mean that workers and their families should suffer the consequences of these hazards. Brady makes an insightful comparison with the airline industry. By its very nature, air travel also comes with significant hazards. A single error could lead to catastrophe. However, the general public expects air travel to be extremely safe, and it is. Flying is safer than driving. The fundamental difference is that we frame air travel in a way that demands extremely high standards of safety, but we don't frame the mining industry in the same way.

In the language of this chapter, one-dimensional safety limits the frame through which we look at improving safety. The focus on ensuring compliance to achieve an absence of physical harm has reached a point of diminishing returns. The methods we've been using have reached the limit of their capacity.

For people like Travis, the physical risks encountered at work have been well mitigated using a combination of *environmental* and *practice-based* factors. Mandatory PPE and the engineering, guarding, and signposting of the physical environment are examples of environmental factors.

Practice-based factors include identification of critical risks, along with a heavy emphasis on compliance with policies and procedures that guide the way workers interact with high-risk tasks. These factors are comprehensive and widespread, yet the statistics on physical harm are no longer getting any better. Applying more of the same – more procedures, more signs, etc. – is going to have little effect.

Two-dimensional safety, which adds psychosocial harm to the mix, has expanded the frame around safety but is not, so far, stemming the rise in the frequency of psychological injury. This is not surprising, because two-dimensional safety is essentially relying on the same types of initiatives – environmental and practice-based factors – that have long been applied to reducing physical harm. In two-dimensional safety, reduction of psychological harm is often heavily reliant on practice factors: complaint procedures, EAP, and training programs. Environmental factors such as posters and other signage might also be used.

Through a combination of wide-ranging research and over 20 years of diverse experience, we have come to the conclusion that safety culture is a product of four factors: the *environment* and *practices* we've mentioned, along with *leadership* and *people*. The interaction of these components is illustrated in our Safety Culture Model. It is the leadership and people factors that are largely missing from one-dimensional and two-dimensional safety.

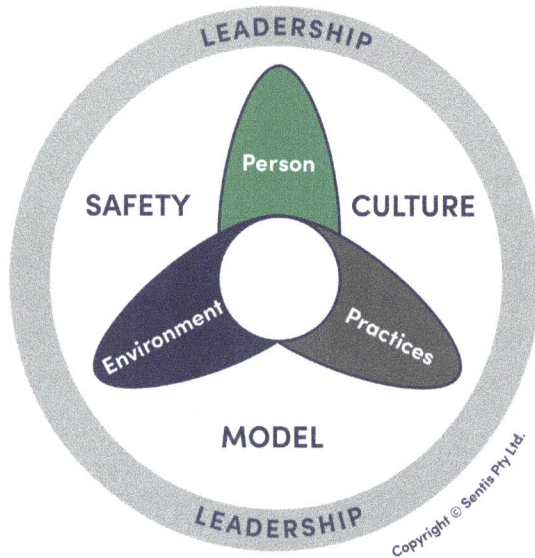

Figure 1 - Safety Culture Model

The person component of safety culture relates to frontline workers and their attitudes and approaches to their own safety and that of their workmates. Their skills, experience, attitudes, intelligence, motivation, behavioural choices, and style of teamwork all come into this. In Julie's case, the attitudes, motivations, and behaviours of some of her colleagues were clearly falling short when it came to psychosocial safety, whether that was through a lack of awareness or because they simply chose to violate the rules.

When it comes to leadership, it is well recognised that the quality and style of leadership has an enormous impact on organisation-wide culture. As the old saying goes, "*a fish rots from the head.*" The link between leadership and safety culture is just as strong. As we delve into the people factor in the chapters that follow, the leadership factor and its impact will be right there with it. The most motivated people in the world won't get far if they aren't actively supported by their leaders.

We believe that the answer to making the next big leap forward in safety lies in taking a holistic view that balances the environmental, practice, people, and leadership factors. This wider view recognises the influence of the physical, social, and psychological experience of the workplace on the ability of our brains to operate optimally. With a deeper understanding of the neuroscience behind optimal human performance and an awareness of the interaction between these three elements of safety, we can make a significant leap forward in achieving safety cultures built upon collaboration.

In summary, we acknowledge the great work that others who came before us have done in the safety space, installing the fundamentals of physical safety management and eventually leaning into assessment and management of the psychosocial safety of work. It's time to step out of the old ways of doing safety that no longer serve us and to adopt a more positive approach to safety that lends itself to building more collaborative and connected workplace cultures that genuinely support people to be safe, well, and engaged.

We will now explore this opportunity in depth, drawing on our own research and that of others, along with real-world examples drawn from the experiences of companies we have worked with. We'll introduce a definition of positive safety and describe the essential work to be done at different leadership levels to achieve more mature levels of safety culture. We'll investigate the role and potential of neuroscience in positive safety.

And finally, we'll offer a leader's playbook for incorporating these ideas, offering practical insights from our own wide-ranging experiences in this space. We hope that by the time you put this book down, you too will be looking at safety in a whole new way.

4.

MOVING TOWARD A POSITIVE SAFETY APPROACH

*"If you want something new,
you have to stop doing something old."*

~ Peter F. Drucker

Crop farming has always been a tough enterprise for those brave enough to undertake it. This is especially the case on a continent like Australia, the *"sunburnt country"* of *"droughts and flooding rains,"* as Dorothea Mackellar put it so vividly in her famous 1908 poem. Even when the conditions are perfect, the promise of a bumper harvest can be ruined by a single untimely hailstorm.

Lawson Grains knows this all too well. The grain farming corporation owns and runs eleven properties covering 120,000 hectares across New South Wales and Western Australia as well as transport and grain storage businesses'.

Aside from the usual environmental hurdles, the vast geographic spread of their properties creates some unique management challenges in terms of achieving a uniform approach to issues like safety. Nevertheless, the company has always been committed to the wellbeing of their people, with safety being central to that commitment. They bring all their staff from across the country together once a year to connect, learn from each other and address safety and cultural issues.

The nature of the agriculture industry is that there are peak times through the year – notably during sowing and harvest – when the risk of fatigue and burnout are high. Taking a proactive approach to this, the company has put strategies in place that encourage their staff to talk openly about these issues. Leaders look for signs of overwork and ensure staff have time off to recover at less onerous times of the year. They were similarly proactive about management of the COVID-19 pandemic and the potential harm to their employees' physical and mental wellbeing.

Lawson Grains recognises the importance of the person and leadership components of the Safety Culture Model. They constantly invest in training at all levels to reinforce these. For instance, resilience training gave leaders a framework to enable them to have effective check-in conversations. Similar training for their teams gave people permission to discuss the stressors and challenges they faced, both personal and work-related. Leaders became more aware of how the stress levels and wellbeing of their team members affected their work. They became more curious and compassionate, while their team members felt more comfortable speaking up.

As a result of their approach to safety, Lawson Grains found that more incidents were being reported and people were openly reporting damaged equipment or faulty machines. Previously their inclination had been to resist doing this; it doesn't come naturally to many employees who have come off family farms. The typical farming mindset is to be action oriented, to find solutions, to 'get it done' – anything but leave a tractor stranded in a paddock and part of a crop unharvested. Many Lawson Grains employees found it hard to shake this habit. Instead, they just kept their workarounds to themselves because they knew they shouldn't be using them. Moving past this meant the underlying issues could be heard and addressed.

Management figured that if an issue was turning up on one property, it likely also existed at some of the others. Knowing that they wouldn't be ignored or punished for raising a problem, team members came to see reporting issues as a way of looking out for each other and preventing injuries, both on their assigned property and all across the Lawson Grains portfolio.

Lawson Grains is an example of a very different approach to safety to what we've been discussing to this point. By emphasising the leadership and people as much as environment and practices, the company has built a holistic, *positive* safety culture that enhances physical, psychological, and social safety across its geographically dispersed business. Far from feeling intimidated by safety initiatives, their people experience safety in a way that makes them feel secure, well, and engaged, while the leadership team exhibits genuine care and support for its people. The whole organisation is continuously improving its approach to safety.

Safety through a positive lens

What if you were able to apply a positive, forward-thinking attitude to the way you manage safety, and in doing so create a positive safety culture in which every person on a site is safe, well, and engaged? What might that look like for your organisation? Is it even viable? The answer to that last question is "*Yes*," without any doubt. We know because we've seen it and experienced cultures like this ourselves.

What we see when we work with positive safety cultures are management attitudes in which people are regarded as the solution, not the problem. In these cultures, managers see themselves not as schoolmasters but as enablers who work with their workforce to optimise safety now and continually improve it in the future. Frontline workers see themselves as part of the 'family' of the organisation, believing that the company has their best interests at heart while also understanding that they have an active role to play in their own safety and that of their workmates. The overriding attitude is of mutual support to a mutually beneficial end.

The behaviours that arise from these attitudes are all about cooperation rather than conflict. In workplaces displaying a positive safety culture like this, there is open and transparent communication up and down the chain, with a willingness to learn from others. Near misses or injuries are investigated in a non-judgmental, non-blaming way, with a genuine interest in the 'Why?' and the opportunity for lessons to be learnt. Managers act as coaches and enablers who are there to support people to do their best work.

Positive safety cultures generally lead to fewer injuries and lost-time incidents, while also constantly seeking to improve. Everyone plays a part in this improvement. Safety is not imposed on anyone – but it is everyone's responsibility. It's not separate from the work – it's part of the work.

Now, you might be thinking that this all sounds a bit idealistic and out of touch with the real world. In the real world, accidents happen. When they do, they're unexpected and unfortunate – the very definition of 'accident'. Occasionally, someone is injured as a result, and that is definitely unfortunate. "*That's life,*" we hear you say, and it's accepted that as long as you're doing all you can to minimise that risk, that's pretty much all you can do.

We beg to differ. This description of a positive safety culture may sound overly optimistic. And given the data in our research, it may well be a long way from what is going on in your organisation right now. But there are many steps of improvement between a stagnant, negative culture and the ideal. The journey to improvement starts with taking the first of those steps. We promise it's worth it.

Adding the third dimension: focusing on the safety experience

As we mentioned at the end of the last chapter, the next big step towards a positive safety culture requires you to adopt a holistic view of safety management. While two-dimensional safety, with its recognition of psychosocial safety, represents progress over the traditional one-dimensional focus on physical safety alone, it still treats the psychosocial experience of work as something separate from the physical experience, while still attempting to manage it using similar, often outdated approaches.

Positive safety requires a more integrated approach to safety that focuses less on numerical outcomes and more on each worker's three-dimensional *experience* of safety, those dimensions being the physical, the social and the psychological. Ultimately, positive safety involves developing and enhancing these three dimensions of the safety experience as a whole.

Figure 2 - The three dimensions of the safety experience

Positive safety recognises the interplay between your physical experience of the workplace, the social experience of interacting with the people around you, and the psychological experience of your internal world. These areas are interrelated. Positive and negative experiences in any of these areas can affect an individual's overall wellbeing, safety, and work outcomes.

- The *physical experience* of safety relates to the way in which you experience the physical environment of your job and your workplace. This includes the tangible aspects of physical safety so central to traditional approaches – the environment itself (e.g. organisation, tidiness, lighting, temperature, noise levels), PPE, level of physical risk, and so on – along with day-to-day aspects of the job such as processes and procedures, shift work, etc.

- The *social experience* of safety relates to your interactions with others in your workplace. This includes everything from the quality of the relationships you have with those around you, the sense of community and the enjoyment you get from your interactions, to the effectiveness of communication and a sense of what is going on, and the willingness of people to solve problems collaboratively and share responsibility for each other's welfare. A strong social experience indicates a culture of trust, in which people feel included and invited to contribute, and everyone looks out for each other. Enhancing the social experience is key to making safety a collective responsibility, rather than an individual one.

- The *psychological experience* of safety is more individual, as it relates to the internal thoughts you have about your work, your ability to meet the expectations of your role, your sense of wellbeing, your stress levels and resilience and your mental health. A positive psychological experience is fostered by a supportive environment in which workers feel engaged, valued, and clear about their responsibilities, and in which stress is minimised and job satisfaction is high.

When you look at safety in this way – as the interaction between the physical, social, and psychological, it becomes clearer why traditional safety initiatives appear to have reached the limit of their capability to reduce harm. For example, if an organisation has invested heavily in the physical work environment, but hasn't prioritised workforce engagement, leadership and inclusive behaviours, their safety performance is likely to have stagnated or continued to fluctuate.

If you think once again about the story of Julie's experience in the mine, her physical safety experience was generally positive. Her risk of being physically harmed while performing work tasks was relatively low because her employer placed a high priority on physical safety. She worked in an air-conditioned vehicle cabin in a well-maintained truck, and she was provided with training and processes to safely perform every task necessary for her role.

However, her social experience was often negative, and her interactions with many of the men were always guarded, tense, and primed to cope with possible abuse, disrespect, or sexual harassment. She definitely did not have a positive psychological experience of safety. Her stress levels were high due to continually being on guard, and she had feelings of frustration at being discouraged from voicing her thoughts and opinions.

The experiences you have in the workplace impact the frames you have around safety. For Julie, feeling so socially threatened and psychologically isolated and unsupported is likely to have left her feeling that she was on her own when it comes to safety, even within a work context that was ostensibly very 'safety conscious'. She was therefore unlikely to report incidents and near misses; she was unlikely to have felt confident enough to speak up or raise safety concerns; she would have started to feel compelled to walk past unsafe acts and turn a blind eye.

Many people find themselves in similar situations, working in organisations that purport to value safety above all else, yet working under a crippling amount of pressure, having little autonomy in their roles, pushed to meet ever-increasing production and output targets, or suffering under toxic team cultures or bullying leadership tactics. In short, negative experiences across the physical, social, and psychological domains can dissolve trust and cause disengagement, and this has dire repercussions for safety.

When a company becomes invested in the three-dimensional safety experience people have within the workplace – when they feel safe physically, socially, and psychologically – then they are more likely to be resilient and reliable. They have space and capacity to grow, and they are more likely to be motivated to collaborate, put in discretionary effort, and contribute to further improvement.

Had Julie's employer taken this more holistic approach, they would still have minimised the risk of physical harm to Julie and her colleagues while also improving their psychological and social experiences. This would have bolstered the overall culture and performance of the site. They might then have enjoyed many years of valuable contribution from Julie as a long-term employee.

The safety experience in practice

In 2023, we analysed a sample of almost 30,000 responses provided to our Safety Climate Survey. Respondents came from workers across 12 industries and 15 countries. The aim of our analysis was to differentiate between participants' physical, social, and psychological experiences at work, drawn from their responses to over 100 Safety Climate Survey items. We wanted to understand their perceptions of their organisation across all three experiences.

The top five strengths identified by participants were all found in the social experience of safety. The positive trends we identified relate to strong feelings of support for safety within the team as well as firm connection with supervisors. This points to strong bonds and collaboration within teams and indicates a positive social experience for most respondents at the team level.

Many employees shared positive perceptions that safety is everyone's duty to maintain, feelings that people look out for each other's safety and wellbeing, and expectations that everyone works safely at all times. Employees also reported positive working relationships with their supervisors and a perception that people are comfortable talking about safety and wellbeing with their supervisors.

Interestingly, four of the top five areas of opportunity identified by participants also related to the social experience of safety. These differed from the positive perceptions in that they did not relate to the social support provided by the immediate team and supervisor. Instead, they related to activities at the organisational or leadership level, such as the management of mistakes, consideration of employees' input in decision making, the recognition of safe behaviour, and the communication of change.

The only opportunity that was not linked to the social experience was the occurrence of regular emergency drills, which relates to the physical experience. It received a negative average score across employees.

Why is it that the most positive and the most negative perceptions of safety climate items are found in the social experience of safety? This is fairly typical of a trend we have observed across our various culture and climate diagnostics. Strong within-team results indicate that employees often perceive their co-workers as supportive and focused on safety. Within their own team, many workers feel that trust is high and communication is effective. They often also feel they can be honest with their supervisors, believing that their supervisors care for their safety.

However, workers often express more negative perceptions of how safety is managed at the organisational level. This is particularly apparent when it comes to rating the effectiveness of incident investigations, reward and recognition programs and communication regarding changes.

In short, the social experience of safety is the area with both the greatest room for improvement and the greatest strengths. If an organisation can strengthen the social experience for workers by improving communication, increasing collaboration, and using mistakes as a platform for learning and improvement (as opposed to punishment and fear), it will be well on its way to improving its workplace culture.

Something worth noting out of this analysis is that all results – even those most positive – were in the 'fair' range on average. This is consistent with the high proportion of negative safety cultures identified through our research. None of the social, physical, or psychological experiences were universally, or even in a large majority, considered strengths contributing favourably to safety performance. Overall, employees perceived opportunities to improve safety across all three experiences.

It is also interesting that the physical experience of safety was not rated more highly. This is the 'traditional' experience of safety, centred around tangible physical equipment: PPE, barricades, equipment, technology, machinery, and environmental design. As we have discussed, this is traditionally the area of safety that receives the most attention and the most spending. Yet our research suggests that despite this disproportionate attention, the physical experience is not necessarily felt positively.

It is likely, given the overlap of the physical, social, and psychological experiences, that a lack of psychosocial support within an organisation contributes to this by dampening the perception of physical safety: "*I might **be** physically safe, but I don't **feel** physically safe.*"

Perhaps less surprising was a slightly lower overall result for the psychological experience of safety, given the more recent acknowledgement of psychological harm as a real concern. While it has formed part of the safety definition for a number of years, at the coalface, psychological safety has only recently started to receive practical attention due to new regulations and global standards, along with an increasing number of workers' compensation claims. Improving the psychological experience of safety is a considerable opportunity for many organisations.[18]

The positive safety continuum: moving beyond compliance

Obviously, the attitudes and behaviours around safety identified in our research varied markedly from one site to another and from one company to another – even amongst those 66 sites that displayed negative safety cultures. Some sites we surveyed were operating at very low, if any, levels of compliance with even the most basic safety protocols. On such sites, both management and the workforce routinely gave minimum attention to safety, and what attention they did give was to physical safety; psychosocial safety wasn't even on the radar.

---

18 Access detail on this analysis in the Unpacking Safety Experiences: Employee Perceptions of Safety Climate (2024) report from the List of Resources at the end of the book.

Other sites in this category operated at much higher compliance levels; however, this compliance is still at the negative end, as these sites are what we describe as 'public' compliance, that is, it relies on being observed or policed. People do the right thing, but only if they're being watched, like drivers who stick to the speed limit only when they know there are police radars around. We can illustrate this variation as being on a continuum from non-compliance to compliance.

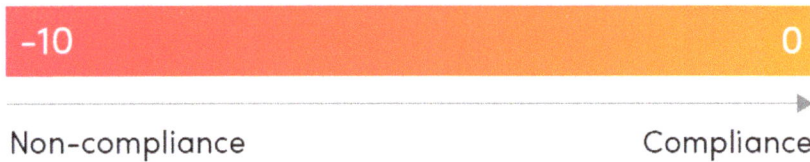

Figure 3 – Non-compliance to compliance continuum

A fundamental aspect of sites operating on this continuum is a focus on an *absence of harm* – usually a one-dimensional focus on the absence of physical harm.

Superficially, this is obviously a good thing. No one getting hurt is what you want, right? The problem is that focusing exclusively on the absence of harm, dependent on compliance, is very limiting. As we know from the statistics, it leads, in practice, to a limit on how much harm can be avoided. Researchers at the University of Aberdeen have drawn the same conclusion. "*Compliance with safety rules and regulations is influential in lowering the risk of accidents. However, safety researchers have realised that in order to achieve high safety levels, mere compliance is not sufficient.*"[19] Safety improves, but only to the point that people are complying with the core safety behaviours.

Positive safety moves beyond public compliance and into a whole new domain. Rather than seeing compliance and the absence of harm as the ideal, positive safety focuses on the 'presence of safety' through its attention to the three dimensions of the safety experience. What we call *private*

19 Shama Didla, Kathryn Mearns & Rhona Flin (2009) Safety citizenship behaviour: a proactive approach to risk management, Journal of Risk Research, 12:3-4, 475-483, DOI: 10.1080/13669870903041433

compliance (compliance regardless of whether anyone is watching) is seen as the minimum. As the safety experience improves, people's perceptions of the safety climate also improve. We start to see behaviours consistent with the collaborative and high-trust state of *safety citizenship*, which is the ultimate goal. We will expand on these terms in a moment.

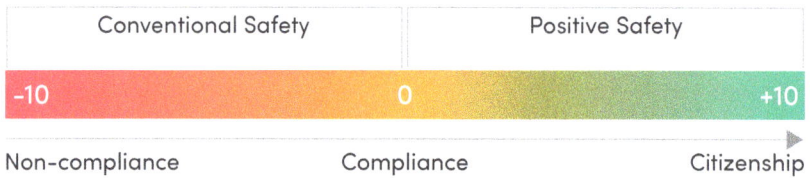

Conventional Safety	Positive Safety
-10	0 +10
Non-compliance	Compliance Citizenship

Figure 4 – The positive safety continuum

Common to all levels of positive safety is genuine commitment to safety by workers and leadership and everyone in between. There is no 'compliance only when you're looking', and neither is there a 'blame the worker' attitude.

Safety culture maturity: a journey to safety citizenship

There is clearly a stark contrast between the approach to safety and the employees' experience of safety when comparing the situations at Julie's mining company and at Lawson Grains.

In short, the mining site represents a negative safety culture in which command and control rule, management wields power over employees, safety is defined purely by public compliance and absence of physical harm, and reporting is motivated by reporting acceptable KPIs. The mine relies heavily on the environmental and practices components of the Safety Culture Model we introduced in the last chapter. Less attention is given to the people and leadership components of that model. As a consequence, the mine sits towards the left-hand 'non-compliance' end of the safety continuum.

In contrast, Lawson Grains represents a positive safety culture sitting towards the ideal right-hand 'citizenship' end of the continuum. Characterised by care and collaboration and shared responsibility between management and staff, safety for this company is defined in terms of the three dimensions of the safety experience: social belonging and psychological health in addition to physical wellbeing. The primary motivation is bringing out the best in the team. Lawson Grains has well-developed people and leadership components of the Safety Culture Model in addition to the environmental and practices components.

As the continuum suggests, a wide range of potential safety cultures exists between these two extremes, with a traditionally effective safety culture built around public compliance and physical safety sitting towards the centre. As we've shown, while such a culture can be successful, the ultimate level of that success will be limited. There will come a point where the number of people being harmed is no longer growing, but it isn't falling either.

In safety cultures operating towards the citizenship end of the spectrum, safety is so well integrated into the business's practices and thinking that an outsider could be forgiven for wondering whether it is thought about at all. This is not, as you might think, a negative. It simply means that safety is ubiquitous and that there is a shared understanding of safety's role in allowing everyone to return home safely at the end of the day. In more mature safety cultures, people engage in safe attitudes and behaviours almost without even thinking about it. People naturally want to contribute more in an environment where they feel a sense of belonging, care, and community.

As businesses move towards citizenship, safety isn't compromised when times get tough, or when the pressure is on. There is no acceptance that 'we've done safety', that we've 'ticked the box', just because the safety procedures are in order. Rather, it's all about continuous improvement, with everyone, at every level, constantly looking out for opportunities to improve. Everyone, at every level, actively chooses to follow safety procedures because they want to, not because they have to. Similarly, they see safety systems as tools that improve their jobs, not inconveniences or barriers to getting the work done.

The Safety Culture Maturity Model

In our work, we expand the concept of a compliance continuum to define five developmental stages of safety culture 'maturity'. We developed the 'Safety Culture Maturity Model' to describe in greater detail the journey organisations take as they progress towards a positive safety culture.

As organisations broaden their definition of safety to better incorporate the social and psychological experiences and as they put greater emphasis on the people and leadership components of the Safety Culture Model, they open up the potential to move towards a positive safety culture. Initially, this might incorporate self-motivated or private compliance. With further development, it might progress to what we call a 'collaborative' safety culture and, ultimately, safety 'citizenship'. Each stage represents a different level of maturity in an organisation's approach to workplace safety.

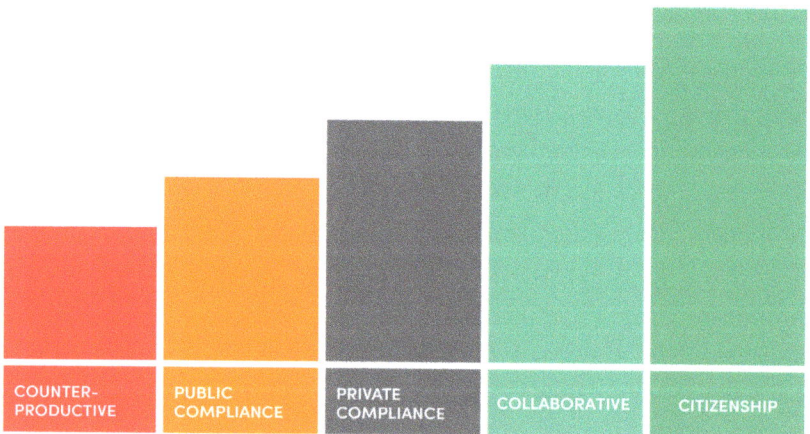

COUNTER-PRODUCTIVE | PUBLIC COMPLIANCE | PRIVATE COMPLIANCE | COLLABORATIVE | CITIZENSHIP

Figure 5 – The Sentis Safety Culture Maturity Model

In counterproductive safety cultures at the lower end of the scale, the approach to safety is often begrudging. Inasmuch as it is given consideration at all, safety is regarded only in the one-dimensional sense of physical harm. Mostly, it is viewed as a cumbersome obligation, a red-tape wrapped, externally-imposed obstacle to getting the real work done. Instead of enhancing safety, the established norms, attitudes, and behaviours contribute to increased risks and complacency.

A counterproductive safety culture is usually characterised by a lack of commitment to safety from the very top of the organisation. Adherence to even the most basic safety norms, such as wearing protective equipment, is inconsistent and poorly monitored. Where there is any compliance, it is with legal requirements – little or nothing more. All of this signals to the workforce that productivity is the priority over safety. This often leads to a pattern of eroded trust within the organisation, with workers looking after their own interests first and the idea of collective goals running a distant second.

At the public compliance level of safety culture, safety is given higher priority, at least visibly. The focus at this level will likely be two-dimensional, with physical safety the responsibility of Health, Safety, and Environment (HSE) and psychosocial safety the responsibility of HR. Overall, however, safety still isn't integrated into the work but rather seen as something *additional to* the work.

Safety is still seen by many as something that gets in the way of getting the job done. Safety is something done to you, not *by* you or *for* you, so it becomes about being compliant only when someone is watching. The thinking is along the lines of: "*When management turn their heads, we'll cut corners if it means we can get our work done more quickly or comfortably.*"

For supervisors and middle management, it's easier to turn a blind eye than to report an incident or a near miss because they know senior management doesn't want to hear bad news or have their figures looking bad. Psychosocial harm is managed using the sorts of after-the-fact tertiary intervention we saw in Julie's story, but there is little proactive action taken to eliminate the risks or alter the safety experience landscape.

Conversely, organisations boasting a well-developed collaborative or citizenship-level safety culture are characterised by individuals making conscious choices to go above and beyond the duties of their role to improve safety for everyone. Safety is seen through the lens of physical, social, and psychological experiences, and there is recognition of the way people and systems work together.

It is also regarded as a core part of everyone's job, a shared responsibility – both in intention and, most importantly, in practice. It is built on a broader culture in which relationships are characterised by high levels of trust and mutual respect. For such organisations, the safety experience isn't an afterthought or something separate from the 'real work'. It is a foundational business principle, prompting individuals to go the extra mile, not just in their roles, but in championing the organisation's overall safety objectives.

Of course, we would like to see all organisations operating at the collaborative and citizenship levels of safety culture maturity. At these levels, safety is prioritised and maintained at the highest levels possible, regardless of any internal and external challenges that might be going on. Leaders encourage participation and empower their workers to be involved with job planning and improvement, and they have strong positive relationships with their individual team members and care about their general wellbeing. The workforce feels psychologically safe to speak openly about safety concerns without fear of retribution, facilitating open and transparent reporting and continuous improvement.

It's safety at the 'citizenship' level, where safety no longer sits out on its own, to the side of the 'real business' but is instead a core part of everyone's job and a genuinely shared responsibility. What we see is that the more mature an organisation's safety culture is, the less talk there is of safety as a 'priority'. It is simply a lived value, synonymous with the company's focus on quality and professionalism.

Challenging the frame that a positive safety approach is 'too soft'

When we run webinars and training events on the topic of positive safety, we encourage our participants to ask their burning questions. Often, participants ask, *"How do I challenge the frame that this approach is 'too soft'?"* and *"How can I get leaders to buy into the importance of psychosocial safety?"*

Taking a positive safety approach and becoming invested in understanding and improving the safety experience of the worker certainly deviates from the way safety used to be done. People's brains are hardwired to resist change, and so, for some, adding the psychological and social lenses to the traditional physical dimension of safety feels overwhelming. It warrants a good reason for committing the effort that is required to change.

Perhaps a poignant way to visualise the necessity of leading a positive safety approach in your organisation is to draw a parallel to Gallup's workplace engagement research. The 2023 results[20] indicate that just over 20% of an organisation's workforce is likely to be highly engaged and 'thriving at work'. These are your top performers, the ones who take pride in the work they do and are most likely to already be going the extra mile and demonstrating organisational citizenship behaviours.

The roughly 60% of workers who are barely engaged make up the majority of the workforce who do their jobs but no more, essentially filling a seat and watching the clock, flying under the radar while doing the bare minimum. Gallup calls these the 'quiet quitters'. Finally, there is a group of approximately 20% of the

---

20 Gallup, *State of the Global Workplace 2023 Report*, 2023, Accessed at https://www.gallup.com/workplace/349484/state-of-the-global-workplace.aspx

workforce who are actively disengaged – the 'loud quitters', if you will. These people lack trust in leaders and are quite disconnected from the organisational objectives.

Worker engagement is relevant because expectations of the workplace have shifted around the globe. People are no longer content to work for their pay while accepting any old conditions that come with it. They want to feel valued and recognised; they want to be challenged and have the opportunity to learn and grow; they want to work with a supportive leader in a healthy team environment. What they are expecting is a positive physical, social, and psychological experience of the workplace.

The risk for organisations is that failing to provide a positive work environment can cause high turnover. And unfortunately, the people most inclined to leave in search of better working conditions will be your top performing workers with the highest employment prospects. It is worth considering the impact this is likely to have: namely, that the proportion of engagement in your organisation will tip towards the *actively disengaged*. The ramifications of this can be significant. In our view, there is nothing remotely 'soft' about striving to be a great place to work, with leaders who are focused on bringing out the best in their people. Leaning into a positive safety approach is not soft… it's smart business.

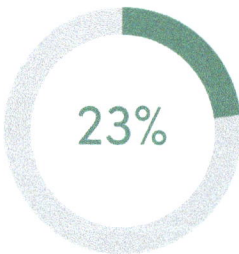

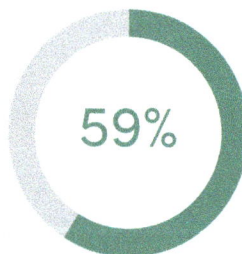

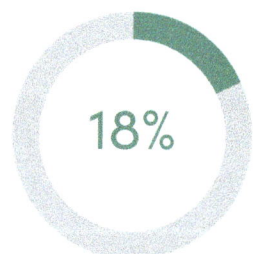

Thriving at work
(Engaged)

Quiet quitting
(Not engaged)

Loud quitting
(Actively disengaged)

Hopefully, it is clear at this point that a positive safety culture is something worth pursuing, and that it can provide benefits much broader than just safety by playing an active role in improving relationships, communication, and productivity all round.

However, while safety citizenship is the ultimate goal, we need to acknowledge that achieving a safety culture at this level takes a substantial amount of work – it won't happen overnight and it won't happen without an ongoing, concerted effort. Recall that in our research, a full 86% of the sites surveyed were operating negative safety cultures, at the 'public compliance' level or below – at least four levels below our gold standard of safety citizenship.

Therefore, for most organisations, the first goal is to reach the 'private compliance' level, which is the foundation of a positive safety culture. It may not look it, but even the move from public to private compliance can be challenging, for it involves one fundamental change: the creation of the intrinsic, internal motivation to act safely at work, *even when no one is watching*.

Achieving this change requires that the interplay between physical, social, and psychological safety is well understood, with the approach to each being deliberately designed. Let's look at how you can establish this vital foundation for your company to build upon, starting with an exploration of the neuroscience behind positive safety.

5.

COMPLIANCE, THE BRAIN, AND MOTIVATION

*"When I hear myself speak,
I learn what I believe."*

~ William Miller

We'll start this chapter with the story of Grace, the safety manager at a large manufacturer. She started with the company a few months ago, employed as part of a concerted effort by a new leadership team to improve safety performance, which had plateaued in recent years.

From the outset, Grace had found the plant well set up in terms of its environmental and practices factors. At first glance, the place *looked* safe, and when she conducted a safety audit it revealed up-to-date risk assessments and policies. When she dropped in on toolbox meetings, safety was often on the agenda. It wasn't immediately obvious where improvements could be made.

Then, one day, Grace walked into the machine shop, unannounced. As she did so, she came upon two fitters standing at a bench with an open first-aid box in front of them. One of them was wrapping a bandage around the finger of the other.

"*Hi Grace,*" said Darren, the injured man, as he noticed her. "*Bit of a nick on my finger. Nothing to worry about. My fault – I took my glove off for a moment to tighten a nut that was hard to get at.*"

Grace could see blood coming through the bandage and suspected the cut was worse than he was letting on. "*I think you should go and see the nurse,*" she said. "*I'll be right. I'll go and see her on my lunch break.*" Darren shrugged it off.

It was only 20 minutes until the break, so Grace figured that sounded reasonable. However, when she saw the nurse in the tea room later in the day, the nurse commented that she'd had a quiet day without a single visitor.

"*You didn't see Darren, the fitter, with a cut finger?*" said Grace. "*Nope,*" said the nurse. "*But by the look on your face, I should have.*" By now it was past the shift changeover, so it was the next day before Grace could go and see Darren again. "*How's the finger?*" she asked. "*A bit sore,*" he said. Looking sheepish, he admitted, "*It didn't stop bleeding, so I went to my GP who ended up putting in a couple of stitches. And before you say anything, I know I should have gone to the nurse but I didn't think it was that bad.*"

Over the next few minutes, Grace was able to extract from Darren the real reasons why he'd avoided going to the nurse: it would have meant reporting an injury, which would have meant admitting that he'd broken a safety rule by removing his gloves, and messing up the perfect 'zero' score the machine shop had reported so far in the month.

"*That would have made me the bad guy in the place for weeks,*" he muttered. "*Maybe the new guy's different, but the old plant manager would have given me a right-royal bawling out and blamed my supervisor as well. Far better to keep it to myself and just get on with the job."*

All of a sudden, the penny dropped for Grace. If Darren was typical, and she suspected he was, there were probably a lot more injuries or near misses occurring than she knew about. Perhaps more importantly, this got to the heart of the plateau in safety performance. Grace realised that an opportunity had been revealed to her that could help her make a real difference. But first, she was going to have to get inside people's brains.

This story is a great example of how one-dimensional safety, with its assumption that ensuring compliance is the way to achieving zero harm, consistently falls short of this goal in practice.

Compliance with safety processes and procedures is, of course, necessary at any level of safety culture maturity. It represents becoming aware of hazards and risks relevant to the workplace that could harm people and adhering to regulations and procedures to mitigate them. Compliance with safety practices is the stable platform from which to launch a journey towards safety citizenship, and it remains foundational to that journey. The problem arises when you rely solely on compliance in order for your safety protocols to work.

As you have seen, and Darren's story is a good example among many, compliance can get you only so far. Even with everyone in the business following the rules and observing the correct protocols, you cannot realise your best safety performance potential with compliance alone. The injury and fatality statistics and research we have shared reinforce this limitation.

Darren's previous bosses believed they had a good safety culture because they rarely saw anyone breaking the safety rules, and their KPIs around incidents and injuries were consistently low. They ruled by command and control, so they knew that if anyone was caught doing something non-compliant, the culprit and their workmates would know about it. But that strong safety culture was a facade, hidden behind public compliance.

As soon as Darren found himself in a spot of difficulty and he knew no one was looking, he whipped off his gloves to make tightening that nut a bit easier… and injured himself in the process. Had Grace not come across him while his mate was applying a bandage, she would have been none the wiser and incidents like Darren's would have been repeated, unnoticed.

The traditional one-dimensional approach to safety that Darren was used to was focused on the *results* the company wanted to achieve (e.g. zero harm) and an assumption that the best way to achieve these results was by managing the *behaviours* they wanted to see in the team members (forced compliance).

The problem with this approach is that it ignores the complexities of human nature. It overlooks a critical aspect of human behaviour: that people's behaviours are driven not by what they are told to do but by their *attitudes*. This is the ABR model – it describes the way in which the outcomes leaders get all stem from the way their people think and feel.

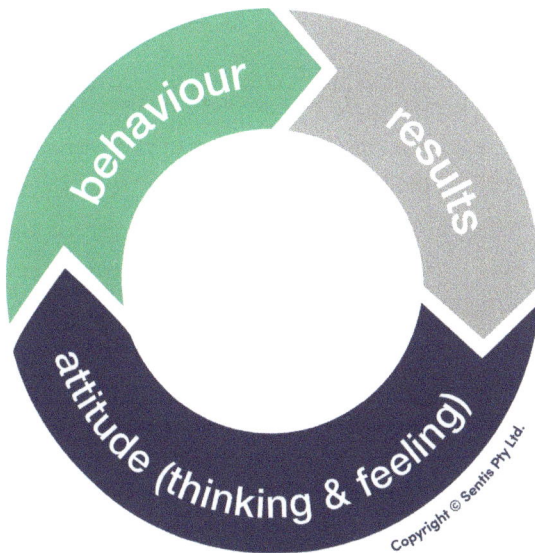

Figure 6 - ABR model – attitude, behaviour, results

It follows that if you want to be successful at driving certain behaviours, you need to be thinking about how your people are thinking and feeling. That means understanding the way people's brains are wired and the sources and quality of their motivations. When leaders fail to understand this, they end up with situations that see people like Darren behaving in ways that might seem illogical – both against their own interests and at odds with established safety protocols.

If you are serious about building a positive safety culture, you need to be able to work within the limitations – and explore the potential – of the brain and its motivations, and the ways in which your people's physical, social, and psychological experiences affect these.

States of the brain

Despite the immense differences between humans' modern lives and those of our hunter-gatherer ancestors, the human brain is more or less the same organ it always was.

First and foremost, the human brain is like other animals' brains in that its first priority is to keep us safe and alive. In order to do this, it has to be aware of danger and respond to physical threats. The 'primal brain' contains the brain stem, limbic region, and the amygdala. This instinctive part of the brain is well developed from birth and is responsible for controlling and regulating our basic systems, such as balance, circulation, and respiration, all without us having to think about them.

The primal brain also helps us stay alert and attentive to our surroundings by automatically scanning the environment for danger. So when the primal brain detects a threat, it instantly switches the brain into a 'survival state'. A distress signal is sent to the limbic system, which instantly prepares our bodies to respond to the danger.

We experience a feeling of fear and the physiological 'flight or fight' response is initiated, often before we are even fully conscious of the danger. Our heart rate and blood pressure rise, our muscles tense and our skin becomes cold and sweaty as our brains prepare us to respond to the threat. Whether it is stepping back out of the way of a quickly oncoming car in the city, or jumping back at the sight of a snake in the bush, the process in our brains is the same: it's all about the primal brain managing and responding to physical threats.

You may have heard about this before. What is less well known is that the brain has a remarkably similar way of responding to social threats. Throughout history, we humans have enhanced our chances of survival by collectively sharing things such as resources, knowledge, and workloads. Being connected to and accepted within the social group meant protection. Conversely, isolation or rejection from the social group meant almost certain death. Understanding this is key to comprehending Darren's response to his injury.

The limbic system acts to protect us from perceived social threats[21] – such as ostracism, criticism, or disrespect – in the same way that the brain protects us from physical threats. Interestingly though, the limbic system's responses often arise in *anticipation* of a social threat rather than as a reaction to it. So, worrying about a looming work deadline, focusing on the uncertainty of our job role, or anticipating conflict with workmates are all circumstances that can trigger the primal brain to release a cascade of stress hormones and initiate the fight or flight response.

---

21 In this discussion around the role of the brain, it is difficult in practice to distinguish psychological safety from the psychological and social experience, the two being very closely related. According to Amy Edmondson of the Harvard Business School, psychological safety refers to a shared belief that it is safe to take interpersonal risks in the workplace (e.g., share an idea, raise a concern). This is a widely used definition and one you may already be familiar with. When looking at our safety experiences model, we consider psychological safety to sit at the intersection between the social and psychological experience. This is because psychological safety describes the interaction between the individual (psychological) feelings and reactions and the people around them (social), and the responses of those people when interpersonal risk is taken.

Once the cortex comes back online and we are able to process the situation with higher-level thinking, we are always motivated to make decisions and take action that will move us away from the physical or social threat.

These responses were evident in Darren's reaction to his injury: on the basis of past experiences, he *anticipated* being bawled out by the plant manager and feared being seen as the 'bad guy' amongst his team, potentially leading to shunning and exclusion. These things had made him anxious; he attempted to allay this anxiety by keeping the injury to himself and not reporting the risk. These sorts of reaction and decision-making are typical when someone is operating from the survival state, when their brain is trying to protect them from danger.

A much more optimal brain state to be operating from, particularly in the workplace, is the 'executive state', which is managed by a large area at the front of the brain called the prefrontal cortex. This is the state in which the brain undertakes problem solving, logical reasoning, learning, creativity and so on.

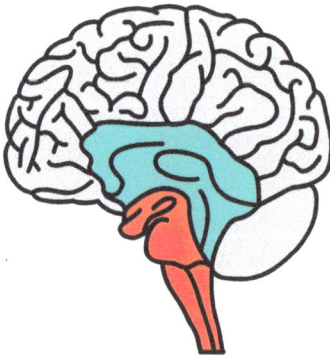

Survival State

Primal brain

The primal brain and limbic system seek to maintain survival by detecting and responding to physical and social threats.

Executive State

Safe, well & engaged brain

The optimal brain state for problem-solving, learning, logical reasoning and creativity.

Figure 7 – The states of the brain

A highly developed executive state is a uniquely human characteristic; however, *we can only engage the executive state when our brains feel 'safe' from physical or social threats.* Conversely, when our brains are preoccupied by threats, our cognitive resources are diverted away from executive tasks, leading to decreased productivity, impaired decision making, and reduced creativity.

Everyone knows this to be true because we have all experienced it. Whether it is anxiety about a relationship, stress about an assignment or upcoming exam, or pressure imposed by a demanding boss, if any of these becomes too much, they can overwhelm our ability to think straight and concentrate on the task at hand.

A logical, 'executive state' response of Darren to his injury would have been to both seek help from the nurse and alert his supervisor to what had happened so that they could find a way to avoid it happening again. But his response was not coming from the executive brain, so it was a self-protective reaction, rather than a reasoned response.

The concept of the executive state becomes particularly relevant to the workplace when we consider ways in which the environments we navigate today are far more complex than those of our hunter-gatherer ancestors. Whether it is crowds of people in a city, artificial light making perpetual daytime out of night or high-speed vehicles moving us along at previously unimaginable speeds, the world is a long way from the natural place the human brain evolved to cope with.

While the brain has made some adaptations, it has had no chance to evolve quickly enough. In an unfriendly environment, we can be confronted with more perceived or real threats than our primitive brains can cope with, causing them to be in a constant state of alertness, compromising our ability to do our jobs productively or safely.

When safety evokes a threat response

Think about this in the context of our manufacturing case study with Grace and Darren.

There were two obvious safety problems with Darren's situation. First, he'd avoided reporting an injury. Second, the reason he had incurred the injury was that he'd removed a glove to make an adjustment, it being too difficult to make the adjustment while wearing it. Rather than report this situation and work with his boss and colleagues to make the situation safer, he pressed on… and cut his finger.

Superficially, neither of these is a rational response. Surely it would be in Darren's best interests to find ways to avoid the injury in the first place and to seek medical care when it did happen. But Darren didn't take that action because of his fears of being yelled at by the plant manager and being socially isolated by his peers. In other words, his brain's survival state overrode its more rational executive state.

Notice that while there was clearly a physical injury risk in this situation, the more motivating factor was the social risk. This led Darren to avoid speaking up about the physical risk and to avoid reporting it when the injury happened. So, while the company had a zero-harm policy, that policy was undermined by a public compliance safety culture in which workers did not feel socially safe to report incidents or risks.

The situation in this example is safety-culture related, but social and psychological risks can arise from broader cultural issues within an organisation. Emotional tensions in the workplace can create a stressful environment, which can directly impact safety. When the threat detector in your brain is activated, your ability to focus on tasks can be compromised, leading to mistakes and accidents.

Imagine that Darren and Grace's plant is going through a bad patch, struggling to meet orders, and having products rejected due to quality issues. The plant manager is under pressure and is struggling to manage his temper as a result. He spends much of his day marching the floor with a frown on his face, pushing his supervisors to speed up and yelling at anyone who makes a mistake.

His negative emotions spread across the floor, and now it's not just Darren whose emotional state is being overloaded, but the emotional state of just about everyone in the plant. The work environment becomes hostile, with everyone on edge, everyone quick to shift blame and no one enjoying themselves. Morale has rarely been lower.

All of this communal stress leads to impaired decision-making, which leads to more mistakes, more quality problems… and more harm, both physical and psychological. A line supervisor, after receiving a particularly aggressive blast from the plant manager, goes off on long-term stress leave, leading to a workers' compensation claim. A machine operator, who is usually diligent about working safely, starts to morally disengage, thinking, *"Why should I follow all these safety rules when the manager doesn't even treat us with respect?"* They start skipping a few safety checks to speed up production, believing that it's justified, given the circumstances. Others do the same and, before long, the injury rate starts to creep up again.

Researchers have found that, accounting for all other variables, moderate and high psychological distress increase the likelihood of having workplace accidents by 40%.[22] That's a sizeable increase.

Of course, there are many other situations that can trigger the reactive survival state. Even in an otherwise healthy environment, if an individual is bullied or harassed, the constant activation of their stress responses can cause them to feel overloaded, which in turn causes their executive functioning to shut down. A single toxic team leader can have a similar effect

---

22 Hilton, M.F. & Whiteford, H.A. (2010). Associations between psychological distress, workplace accidents, workplace failures and workplace successes. International Archives of Occupational and Environmental Health. https://link.springer.com/article/10.1007/s00420-010-0555-x

on a number of people. Interpersonal conflict between two people can diminish the performance of them both.

Whatever the underlying cause and no matter how widespread, it's easy to see how feeling socially and psychologically unsafe can cause workers to disengage from any ideas of being proactive about safety and moving beyond public compliance. They keep their heads down and keep quiet. This is where we come back to people and leadership. While you can provide a sense of physical safety through the use of environmental and practice-based factors, this can only bring safety culture maturity up to the level of public compliance. Integration of the social and psychological experiences is needed to move beyond that.

When the brain feels safe

When Grace realised that changing the safety culture was going to require getting inside people's brains, she was thinking about Darren's psychological and social experiences of the workplace. Darren's reaction to his injury was a symptom of the company's broader safety culture; a culture in which he rarely felt completely safe. The leadership team now had to drive a new culture that would change that.

People have an expectation that when someone is trained and experienced in a role, they will be able to perform that role to the best of their ability. However, the complexity of the brain means that things aren't so straightforward. It's now apparent that someone's experience of the workplace can compromise their ability to stay focused, make good decisions, and work safely.

Every business needs their people's brains to feel safe, simply to perform safety compliance behaviours such as following safety procedures and implementing controls to reduce exposure to hazards. This 'brain safe state' occurs when employees enjoy positive physical, social, and psychological experiences, and their brains are not preoccupied with potential threats.

This allows their cognitive resources to be directed wholly towards undertaking their work efficiently, accurately, and safely. In other words, they have the mental space to be able to do their jobs to the best of their ability. Furthermore, less stress and burnout lead to improved mental health and overall wellbeing, which results in reduced psychological harm, lower absenteeism, and lower turnover.

When people feel socially safe,[23] they are also more likely to engage in open communication and collaboration. They feel comfortable speaking up when mistakes are made because they don't fear being blamed or ostracised. If they come across a potential safety risk, they are more likely to raise it, knowing that their supervisors will likely support them in reducing that risk. They are more willing to share ideas, take calculated risks and learn from mistakes.

More than that, open communication promotes trust and cooperation between team members. This social safety leads to employees being more likely to look out for each other. This leads them to not only sticking to safety protocols, but also going above and beyond expectation, because they want to, *not because someone might be watching.*

In short, when people feel safe, they have more helpful attitudes and better decision-making abilities, they are less likely to be involved in accidents, more likely to report an incident if it does occur, and less likely to be forced off work due to psychological harm. Improved and consistently improving safety performance is the result.

Achieving success in this area requires unlocking the potential to reach the private compliance level of safety culture maturity as a minimum, and then to move beyond compliance and towards safety citizenship. In other words, your business starts moving onto the positive side of our safety continuum, towards a three-dimensional safety experience. In order to influence a workforce to willingly do this, to do more than the minimum because they

---

23 That is, psychologically safe in the terminology used by Amy Edmondson (see previous footnote #20).

want to, not because they have to, you need to understand the motivation for safety.

Understanding motivation

There's another area in which long-held assumptions have contributed to a failure to progress safety cultures beyond the compliance point on the safety continuum, and it has to do with the type and quality of the motivation to act or to behave in certain ways.

When Vincent Kelly and his mates were building the Sydney Harbour Bridge, their motivation for working safely – at least as safely as they knew how and were able to – was pretty simple. One mistake could lead to a serious injury or worse, and if they were hurt or killed, the consequences were all on them. There would be no compensation and no pay for any period off work. So, any safety precautions they took were because they chose to take them – they wanted to take them. Not because anyone told them to (except, perhaps, their wives!), or because they would be punished if they didn't take them, but because they wanted to get home at the end of each day.

This *autonomous*, 'I want to' motivation to be safe probably wasn't something anyone thought about at the time. It was just what you did to survive. And it must have worked to some extent because, as we mentioned earlier, only two of the thousands of men who worked, unharnessed, on the construction of the bridge fell to their deaths from the arch.

Later, as we've seen, the motivation to work safely pushed many workers to the point of leaving their jobs rather than accepting unsafe working conditions. This ultimately led to the introduction of workers' compensation, safety equipment (PPE) and safety procedures.

Then things started to get more complicated. As legislation increasingly shifted the onus for safety onto employers, those employers became more and more stringent about their people using PPE and following processes. In more dangerous industries like mining, being caught without, say, a hard hat on your head became a sackable offence, no questions asked.

With this shift, on most sites the motivation to work safely changed from being autonomous (I want to) to being *controlled* (I *have* to). This shift created some subtle but important changes in the way safety precautions were viewed.

There was increasing reliance on controlled motivation, imposed via a command-and-control style of management, which provided a none-too-subtle implication that safety wasn't something that workers needed to think about. For decades, this became the default approach to safety management, the assumption being that drawing a hard line would prevent anyone straying from it.

The underlying message seemed to be: "*Leave your brain at the gate. Just do as we tell you to do and you'll be safe. (And we won't get sued.)*" This was almost the opposite of what Vincent Kelly had experienced, albeit with a better safety environment and practices in most cases.

However, this reliance on controlled motivation assumed that workers would toe the line. Unfortunately, the truth is that few people enjoy being told what to do. We like to have at least some degree of agency in our decisions about what actions we take, what behaviours we will employ, what we will say, and so on. Our pushback against being dictated to starts pretty much as soon as we realise we can. Think of the infant who refuses to eat and keeps their mouth clamped shut at meal times. The toddler who repeatedly throws their hat on the ground. The teenager who finds subtle ways to make their school uniform not-so-uniform, by hitching up the skirt or choosing an over-sized, untucked shirt. In many cultures, this innate rejection of being controlled - as long as we can get away with it - is ingrained by the time we meet adulthood.

And so, it came to pass in the workplace. Julie discovered colleagues had been smoking in their trucks' cabins. They knew they shouldn't – it was against the rules – but they did it anyway because they could get away with it. The people who bullied Julie knew that it was against company policy, but they also knew, again, that there wouldn't be any consequences. Darren removed his gloves to tighten a nut in the machine shop. He knew he shouldn't but figured no one would notice. He did it again after cutting his finger and then ignoring Grace's suggestion that he go and see the nurse.

Another factor at play here is *extrinsic* motivation, which is where we choose to take an action in order to receive (or avoid) something else. It's the 'What's in it for me?' form of motivation, and it can be very powerful. The basic controlled motivation for Darren to keep his gloves on was extrinsic: by keeping them on, he would avoid any chance of punishment for breaking the rules. But the stronger motivation turned out to be that by removing the gloves he could save time and avoid the hassle of reporting the risk.

It's the same psychology that Lawson Grains' management came up against when trying to encourage members of their team to stop and report any incidents or near misses when they happen rather than continuing to work or fixing the issue without reporting it. Management understands this interplay between different levels of motivation. Their success has been in making reporting a safe and easy path – the path of least resistance – so that their employees understand and are invested in the positive impact that reporting has on other farm employees across the business.

In his extensive research, Dan Pink sheds light on the potentially perilous consequences of motivating people with extrinsic rewards. He points to the ill-fated design and early production of the Ford Pinto in 1971, in which the relentless pursuit of specific production goals led to the oversight of critical safety checks. The result was the production of a car with a flawed and dangerous fuel system design, which burst into flames if the gas tank was damaged in a collision.

Over 27 deaths resulted and the entire fleet of cars had to be recalled in March of that year. This shocking example serves as a powerful metaphor for the workplace, where an exclusive focus on external incentives can lead individuals to choose expedient, often unethical, paths to achieving desired outcomes.

Pink argues that by tethering performance solely to monetary rewards – which is, by definition, a form of extrinsic motivation – companies undermine the inherent drive that arises from genuine interest, personal satisfaction, and a sense of purpose. This myopic fixation on extrinsic rewards diminishes the intrinsic joy derived from tasks, ultimately eroding the passion and commitment that fuel sustained high-level performance.

However, extrinsic motivations aren't always complicated, and they can be associated with autonomous 'I want to' motivations. Some people will happily follow safety protocols for the reason they exist: because the reward is a reduced risk of harm. One of Darren's workmates might have chosen to keep their gloves on in the same situation because they believed that gloves are an effective way of avoiding serious cuts.

Travis might be rigorous about wearing his safety glasses all day, not because he has been told to do so but because he understands and agrees with the proposition that they'll protect his eyesight. Someone else – and these individuals do exist – might follow procedures because they have the value of safe work deeply ingrained in their identity. These are the people who follow the safety instructions on power tools and bags of potting mix in their own homes.

The highest quality and ideal form of safety motivation is *intrinsic* motivation. While extrinsic motivation is about getting one thing in return for another, when we are intrinsically motivated to do something, it is because we actually want to do the thing itself, because we find it interesting, enjoyable, or satisfying. In a safety context, intrinsic motivation looks like joining the safety committee because you value safety and you enjoy working with like-minded others to make things better. Or you help a workmate complete an incident report because you enjoy the camaraderie, care about their wellbeing, and value the idea of making the workplace safer for everyone.

An intrinsically motivated workforce is characteristic of a high level of safety culture maturity. At safety citizenship, workers enjoy positive social and psychological safety experiences, which fosters a collective desire to make their workplace as safe as it can be. Physical experiences are also improved by this shared interest in maintaining the workplace and equipment. Command-and-control management has been left well behind, responsibility for safety having moved from primarily being about management to something shared by all.

Exploring the why

In the description of motivation here, we have presented a number of dichotomies: extrinsic and intrinsic motivations, external and internal motivations, controlled and autonomous motivations. Each of these pairings provides a different insight into a type or source of motivation. It is worth taking a few minutes to understand the way these terms relate to one another and the six levels of motivation quality according to self-determination theory, as applied to occupational safety. In the diagram and list below, the six motivation types are listed from weak to strong motivational quality.

Figure 8 - Types of safety motivation based on self-determination theory (Adapted from Gagné & Deci, 2005; Ryan & Deci, 2002)

1. No motivation for safety

Although rare, we need to acknowledge that some employees in some situations simply cannot be motivated to work safely and are unlikely to engage in appropriate and expected safety behaviours.

Controlled motivation

Controlled 'I have to' motivation for safety can come from either external or internal pressures.

2 External pressures for safety

Safety motivation due to *external pressure* is motivation driven by outside forces rather than internal personal beliefs. It is the most basic form of motivation. Associated behaviours involve complying with safety rules to gain external rewards or avoid punishments. For example, when an employee wears safety goggles to avoid a penalty or to receive a bonus tied to compliance with safety rules, not because they appreciate the benefits of eye protection.

Leaders' note: While motivation due to external pressure can be effective in the short term, it may not lead to long-lasting commitment to safety practices. This is 'carrot and stick motivation', so it requires leaders to be actively, visibly, and constantly overseeing the workplace. Without the threat of punishment or promise of reward, the behaviour quickly disappears.

3 Internal pressures for safety

Safety motivation due to *internal pressure* relates to behaviours driven by guilt or shame. Employees reacting to internal pressure might follow safety procedures to maintain self-esteem or to avoid internal discomfort. As with external pressures, their behaviours still don't reflect a genuine valuing of safety for safety's sake. When a worker diligently wears a harness when working at height because they would feel deeply ashamed if they were caught being the only one not wearing one – as opposed to believing in the potential of the harness to save their life – that is internal pressure at work.

Leaders' note: This form of motivation is still somewhat externally driven, as it's based on how others might perceive the employee. Workers motivated by internal pressures for safety will likely comply with procedures when working with others, but this can't be guaranteed when they are alone and/or not being observed.

Autonomous motivation

Autonomous 'I want to' motivation for safety comes in three levels of quality.

4 Belief in safety

Some construction workers arrive early to a new site and start a hazard assessment because they believe it's essential for their and their teammates' wellbeing. This is an example of belief in safety: the employees following safety rules because they understand, agree with, and value the importance of a safe work environment. They recognise the personal and collective benefits of safety and willingly comply with rules.

Leaders' note: Here, the motivation is more internalised, with the employees seeing the value in the activity itself. As a leader, this is the motivational driver you want to see in your team, as it means you can trust that they will carry out their tasks safely and professionally, whether or not they are being observed.

5 Personal identification with safety

Personal identification with safety reflects safety values that are deeply ingrained in an employee's identity. For people with this level of motivation, safety practices are harmonised with other aspects of their life. They consistently engage in safe behaviours because it aligns with who they are. They do this at home as well as at work, simply because being safe aligns with their self-concept as a responsible and cautious person.

Leaders' note: This is a mature form of motivation, where the values guiding safety behaviours are fully assimilated into the person's identity. These are the people who truly champion safety. They can often have a positive influence on the team around them.

6 Intrinsic motivation for safety

Intrinsic motivation for safety is the most internalised form of motivation. Employees in this category engage in safety activities because they genuinely find them enjoyable, satisfying, or interesting. They don't need any external reward. These are the employees who volunteer for the workplace safety committee because they are passionate about creating a safe environment and find the role intrinsically rewarding and fulfilling.

Leaders' note: While it's true that employees are unlikely to feel much joy from following procedures and engaging in the core safety behaviours, many people do choose to engage in voluntary safety participation behaviours because they find contributing to their team in this way is deeply satisfying and an integral part of their work life.

Moving past the limits of compliance

Ensuring compliance has been the core of safety management for a long time. And we know that it has worked… to a point. But that's the problem. Just because you achieve a high level of compliance doesn't mean you don't have a negative safety culture.

It is possible for people to comply with rules 99% of the time while at the same time holding negative safety attitudes. It is possible for leaders to be meeting safety and production targets and looking good on paper while, knowingly or unknowingly, cultivating a team atmosphere that hinders trust, collaboration, and innovation. The problem is that as soon as management looks away, that other 1% comes into play and Darren cuts his finger, or worse.

If compliance alone is not enough, the question becomes, "*What can you do to increase the maturity of your safety culture?*"

We'll get into a detailed answer to this question, but in the context of this chapter, the answer boils down to having a positive influence on the way people think and feel. This will engender the sorts of positive attitudes that will drive the behaviours associated with safety citizenship and which result in both willing compliance and the desire to go that extra mile and contribute to a physically, socially, and psychologically safe workplace from a values-driven position of professionalism and care.

This is why understanding people's motivations for safety is so critical. You will only see safety citizenship behaviours when people can shift out of controlled motivation and into autonomous motivation – when they want to contribute to a safe and positive workplace because they want to invest in their own health and wellbeing, and because they care about the people around them, not because they feel they have to.

That's because people need to feel safe, physically, *and* socially. They need to feel valued enough to make contributions and share their ideas. They need to trust that if they speak up about a safety hazard, they will be taken seriously and something will actually change. They need to know that if they tag out a machine for safety reasons, they won't get their butt kicked for stopping production. They need to believe that their supervisor and their workmates have their back, and that their senior leaders care as much about the wellbeing of their people as they do about the profitability of their company.

All of this is supported by our research into safety culture and safety climate, which reveals a strong correlation between physical, social, and psychological experiences of safety and safety citizenship behaviours. Notably, the strongest correlation with safety citizenship behaviours was not the physical experience of safety, the area of traditional focus; it was the social experience of safety.

A positive social experience score is also likely to mean more willingness by the workforce to go above and beyond public compliance in order to improve safety and support the safety of others. Creating a positive social culture and supportive team environment is likely to drive more positive safety behaviours by team members.

Let's now turn our attention to what leaders at all levels can do to foster a positive safety culture.

6.
EIGHT PRINCIPLES OF POSITIVE SAFETY

"A true teacher would never tell you what to do.
But they would give you the knowledge
with which you could decide what
would be best for you to do."

~ Christopher Pike

The eight principles of positive safety lay the foundation for a culture based on positive safety. These will apply differently at different levels of leadership, but they each have relevance, which we will explore in further detail. First though, we'll introduce the principles and allow some of the people we've worked with to show how they have applied them. We'll also draw in some points from other prominent people in the safety industry, illustrating a number of findings consistent with our principles.

Principle 1. Lead with a vision

Having a clear vision for safety that neatly aligns with the organisation's wider vision and mission and promotes the 'why' and 'what's in it for me?' is essential. It provides all stakeholders with clarity and direction on matters of safety. Leaders must live and breathe this vision, drawing on it to guide their decision making, while also linking behaviours, performance, and recognition to the vision and promoting safety as a driver of positive culture change more broadly.

Two of our clients demonstrate the value of vision while coming from quite different contexts.

Lawson Grains was a new business in 2012 when it bought its first property near Moree, in New South Wales. As Robyn Heap, General Manager, People & Safety, tells the story:

> *"In the early days, Russell, our General Manager (and later CEO) travelled a lot and spent a lot of time on the ground with each farm manager. He really set the business up for success in that sense, by building good relationships with the farm managers. He did a lot of work in personal growth and development, as did the entire executive team, through coaching and reflection. Russell's vision and his care for employees was built within the culture."*

The clarity of that vision drives Lawson Grains' mature safety culture. At its heart is a stated and lived value, centred around the wellbeing of its people. *"We are wellbeing first. We act with professionalism, integrity, and respect for our peers, partners, and stakeholders,"* Robyn affirms.

At the other end of the age scale is an organisation that is nearly a century old: Australian Red Cross Lifeblood (formerly the Red Cross Blood Bank). This longevity, along with the clarity of the organisation's mission, is very powerful – something that is recognised by Director of Health, Safety & Wellbeing, David Savio, his colleagues, and the board.

> *"We are very lucky and very fortunate at Lifeblood because we have 90 years of history, strong values, and culture. [We focus on] unlocking our inherent purpose, values, and culture and just being a bit more intentional around those. That's a focus that has come from the board and the executive. [As part of that], psychosocial factors have become*

a fundamental focus for us, and the board chair is always asking questions around our appetite for wellbeing."

This legacy helps David and others maintain the vision across almost 100 blood donation centres spread across Australia: centres small, large, and mobile. However, it does require ongoing work.

"It's important for our leaders to really deeply understand and connect with our values, because they require a very different level of thinking. Rather than just memorising or rote learning the values, it's about being insightful or reflective and being able to use them to navigate ambiguity and challenging situations. As leaders, there's a privilege and a responsibility to be consistently and intentionally communicating the vision and setting clear expectations about people living the values."

David makes a point that nicely sums up the importance of values – to the organisation as a whole as well as to safety.

"If you've got a workforce that expends a lot of energy that isn't directed towards its purpose, then it's inefficient. [On the other hand,] when you can cultivate this energy at the local individual, team, and organisational level, you have this synchronicity, like a flock of birds. There's just this energy that is in sync and helps us drive our opera-tional goals and fulfil our purpose as an organisation."

Principle 2. Build a strong foundation

A holistic view of the safety experience, incorporating the distinction and interaction between the physical, social, and psychological experiences provides a deeper understanding than the less comprehensive one-dimen-sional and two-dimensional versions of safety that came before it. A strong foundation is needed to simultaneously support employees' physical, social, and psychological experiences of safety. That includes leaders having the skills, capability, and capacity needed to engage with the systems that have been provided and to link their people in with those.

Reflecting on his time in mining, Anthony Butcher, now Head of Health, Safety & Wellbeing at Synlait Milk Ltd notes the importance of building a strong foundation for safety by investing in leadership and culture.

"Many businesses find that they talk about safety and focus on safety when everything's running well. But as soon as there's a crisis or there's a change in resource prices or something, all of a sudden it's production over safety. From my experience, however, you have to continue to invest in safety. You don't want to have to find the money when things go wrong, because then you end up paying twice the amount, if not three times. Investing in safety is like maintaining your car – if you look after it, it'll be reliable.

In New Zealand we have the ACC, the Accident Compensation Corporation, which is like the national insurance against accidents, and you pay a levy based on your industry and risk profile. This levy goes into a big pot that the ACC uses to fund treatment and compensate for salary lost etc. Following a significant investment in training and leadership and empowering our people to take initiative and solve problems when it came to safety, we achieved a reduction in injuries and their severity. From this we were able to achieve a 50% discount on our ACC levy, and that equates to hundreds of thousands of dollars saved. We got there by investing in our people and our safety culture."

At Australian Red Cross Lifeblood, David Savio draws on his background in sports science to build this foundation.

"Workplace culture is a lot like that of a sporting team. There's the team, and there's the community that sits around it. Whether it's Collingwood Football Club, or Manchester United, or whatever, they don't try and work out what they can do to avoid harm. They're about premierships, they're about winning.

"So, you can have an amazing player, someone like [retired AFL champion] Buddy Franklin or [Australian women's soccer captain] Sam Kerr, but if you put them in a team environment with no game plan, no clear objectives, and dysfunctional management, well, no matter how amazing they are, they're not going to be able to thrive over time. So, a lot of the work we did, with Sentis' help, was looking at setting the right conditions that support a collaborative environment, ensuring that we cultivate an environment that optimises, and is a precondition for, high performance."

David recognises that there needs to be a focus at the individual level as well. This is where we come to the individual experience.

"At an individual level, people need to have a level of resilience and mental fitness, and we try to influence those as an organisation. We do this, for instance, through promoting awareness of our wellbeing program. We also need to be concerned with the way individuals fit into the social context. The workplace is like an aquarium. If you've got a fish that's unwell, and you remove it to treat it but then put it back into the same toxic environment, it's going to be unwell again. [On the same basis,] if I've got a team that just wants to be mediocre, any star players on that team will eventually want to go to another team – a team that's going to support and challenge them."

Over the last few years, Lawson Grains has worked to build a strong foundation by focusing on strong relationships. Robyn Heap explains:

"At the end of the day, if you've got a crappy relationship, well, you're not really going to function that well at work – that goes for either party. So, we've looked at opportunities to help people foster building relationships. A good example is our annual conference. Years ago, we used to just bombard them with so much information and so much training, it was just a head spin.

"But then we realised that actually, connections and relationships are what it's all about. So now we only have about half the amount of content, and we leave space for downtime, social interactions and doing fun activities together. That's more of our focus now – giving people the time to build and foster their relationships and connections. It might seem hard to do that, but it's not really. It's just a decision that you make, that you find time within people's days, or conferences, or whatever it is, to just have a chat."

New Zealand company Bremworth Ltd, a manufacturer of wool carpets, had to completely rethink the foundations of its business model - literally – after a Cyclone Gabrielle severely impacted the Napier region in early 2023. One of its major manufacturing facilities located in the region experienced significant flooding causing it to go offline. At the time of writing 7 months later*, the company did not have a definitive view of the future of the site and it remained offline. According to Dr Kirstine Hulse, General Manager at the NZ Product Accelerator, this situation has forced the company to "recalibrate in terms of its organisational design and development perspective." Safety is central to this process.

"We are trying to give people an opportunity to grow, putting them into different roles that fit with their needs and career desires. That may not feel like it's a safety focus, but in a sense it is. There's been a lot of stress over these last six months and some people were being really tested to the limit with their roles shifting and their responsibilities quadrupling.

"For some of them, they've had to totally pivot from what they used to do to something completely new, and for some people that's uncomfortable. And so, we are focusing on getting people back into a space where they can thrive and doing that by the design of work and our recalibrated strategy. In this way we set ourselves up for success so that we can continue our focus on our core critical risks management, and so on. We focus on that with collaboration and partnership

* September 2023

amongst our workers, using safety as the vehicle to cement the value of working together."

Prior to the Cyclone, the company already displayed many characteristics of building a strong safety culture. The focus in recruitment, job allocation and training was on *"putting people into places where they are set up to thrive,"* not only in terms of physical safety but also *"the social and psychological experience of each role."* To further quote Hulse:

> *"We are getting structured about not putting people into places where they won't be set up to thrive... We're working on psychological safety, because we want people to be able to connect with their teams, and we are working on our culture to build the capability of our leadership, too. These are not separate things; everything's got to be integrated. I think safety falls over when it's not integrated."*

Another component of a strong safety foundation is the detection and management of critical risks. The Brady Review noted that *"the majority of the 47 fatalities (during the reviewed period of 2000 to 2019) involved at least one failed or absent control that could have prevented the fatality. The underlying factors for these absent controls often stemmed from decisions made at a supervisory and/or organisational level in organisations. In recent years, the role played by ineffective controls in incidents, including serious accidents, is increasing."*

The Brady Review made two recommendations relating to this: First, that the mining industry should focus on ensuring the effectiveness and enforcement of controls to manage hazards and, second, that the industry should adopt the principles of High Reliability Organisational Theory, which in essence means focusing on *"identifying the incidents that are the precursors to larger failures and [using] this information to prevent these failures occurring."*

Principle 3. Actively care

Traditional safety management concerns itself with minimising physical harm, which is obviously a positive thing. From a personal perspective, organisations want each employee to be able to return home to their family after their shift, and from a business perspective they want them to be fit and healthy when they come in to work the next time.

Positive safety goes much further than this by taking an interest in the whole person and their experience of work. Organisations want every employee to enjoy positive physical, social, and psychological experiences in the workplace. They want this for the same reasons: because they care for the people who work for them, and because they know that healthy, happy people do better work.

"I want leaders who are altruistic in a way, who are driven to help people develop and be the best that they can be. I need them to be able to be humble, but also fair. Leadership is a tough job; the expectations on them are high and it is all too easy to burn out.

"But when you get a win and find that you're having an impact – it might be years later someone coming to you and saying they remember you having a conversation with them that really helped them – that's what leadership is for. So go into leadership because you want to make a difference, not because you want the pay packet or the title." – Linda Murry, General Manager, Hay Point Port & Rail, BHP

"We're lucky to have a very strong purpose [at Lifeblood]. But for us to be able to deliver on that work, we need to take care of the people who are employed to do that life-giving work. And so we have an integrated approach: we have proactive care which is focused on prevention, because our work environment is dynamic and highly variable. We look at eliminating or managing foreseeable risk.

"*We also look at the promotion of health and wellbeing, and putting things in place that help inspire behaviours that support physical, cognitive, and emotional wellbeing. We endeavour to understand and optimise those psychosocial factors.*

"*Let me give you a practical example. For the physical work we do, we've eliminated the physical hazards as far as reasonably practical. We also consider the psychosocial hazards – we want the work to be stimulating enough, but not in a context where it puts physical and mental stress on people and overloads them. We are cognisant that it can be emotionally taxing.*

"*Every time a staff member puts on a uniform, there is an emotional load attached with that; there's a privilege and a responsibility that comes with the work that is symbolic of the uniform. And then, of course we have [other stakeholders in] recipients and donors and volunteers and communities. So emotional awareness, management and regulation are really important.*

"*And then there's a cognitive aspect to our work, and we want to ensure the work is stimulating and engaging. So, we do focus on the conditions in the workplace. We try to ensure that work is human centred and supports a good physical, social and psychological experience of the workplace.*" – David Savio

"*Rio Tinto has introduced a 'felt experience' metric across the company. It's about understanding the felt experience of our workforce and the effectiveness of safety rituals, as we see this as being linked to our safety culture maturity. We have reset our expectations on how to lead for both physical and psychological safety. Our leaders have had external training, which is all about connection and collaboration between leaders and teams when navigating change and challenging times, and we have applied this approach to improve our safety rituals.*

"We have 1,500 people on site [at Queensland Alumina] doing hard physical work. Part of our leadership routine is that we have a drumbeat of interacting with those team members for two hours a day. Not like it used to be, where the safety person was like the policeman there to catch you out. We do this at the same time every day so they know we're coming. They know we're there to support them, find out what roadblocks are in their way, give them positive feedback on what's going well.

"If I see a coaching opportunity, I'll have a conversation with them in good faith and from a position of genuine care. What we've found is that regardless of whether an interaction has just been a conversation and recognition for good work, or whether it's been a coaching conversation to improve an aspect of safety, when the superintendent walks away, that person feels valued and cared for." – Craig Wise, Superintendent Safety and Plant Protection, Queensland Alumina Limited (QAL)

"Rather than working on getting better documentation, better risk assessments and all that, we need to focus on how we support the leaders to lead better. You can see the difference. Take a pre-start. One leader has his nose in a clipboard, 'There's going to be a bit of rain today...' well, they're not engaging the crew. Another can just look around the collection of people and know who's switched on and who's off. They then make decisions based on that, from a position of active care.

"Work in refineries can involve a bit of confined space entry [which is potentially dangerous]. A great leader is in tune with their people and might say to someone, 'You're not going into a confined space today, mate. We'll sit you outside over here doing this stuff in the workshop.' When they have that true connection with the team, those supervisors ensure that they're actively caring and not putting these people in harm's way." – David Pope, Safety Strategist

"Safety training shouldn't just be hammering in what a hazard is, what risk is and how to report it. We found that when our leadership programs were very operationally based and focused on safety compliance rather than on people leadership skills, the culture surveys showed issues with low engagement, high turnover, and absenteeism. Your workplace safety clearly isn't great if you have high compliance but all the people metrics aren't doing so well. In the last three years, particularly off the back of COVID, the promotion of leaders has been much less around operational skill and tenure, and we are seeing more leaders who are empathetic and who bring people together." – Bennjamin Mathews, National Health & Safety Strategy and Risk Manager at Kmart and Target Group.

"We had drought in 2018 and 2019, and then we had floods the next year and the year after, then mouse plagues. And then we had COVID on top of all that. We saw the farm teams slog it out in muddy conditions where they could be bogged 20 to 60 times a day. Sometimes they might only get half their farm planted or harvested. Then, in their words, they felt like they'd let the rest of the business down. That's why we've focused a lot on their wellbeing and resilience and mental health. Because even though farmers are a resilient bunch, you can't just be complacent and think, 'They'll be right.' 'She'll be right,' is a big part of the typical farming attitude, but she'll be right until actually, she's not. We don't want to get to the 'not' bit. That's why the whole executive team and our CEO have that care about the farm teams.

"We have the production versus safety conversation a lot, where we send the message that if you're not sure, you always err on the side of safety. So, if you've got a piece of machinery that's faulty, shut it down. We don't want people to push through for harvest with a dodgy piece of equipment just because we've got to get the crop off. We'd rather have some financial loss because the repercussions of having an injury are huge – not only on lost production when work is shut down, but also for our people and the families and communities that depend on them." – Robyn Heap

"I remember a serious incident that occurred quite a few years ago. Two young guys were doing maintenance around the dam of a mining operation, and they were struggling to get a large pump working. The pump was on the back of a trailer and one of guys tripped over hoses on the pump platform, nearly falling into the dam, but instead managed to jump off the other side of the trailer. He fell on a protruding jack handle, and it ended up penetrating right through his leg. He was lucky his offsider was with him, as he called for help, and radioed me to meet them at the emergency centre. When I shared the news with the rest of the team afterwards, I reflected that the first time I met his wife was at the worker's hospital bed. I use this story with my teams to drive that message about what safety means to us. I tell them, I want to be meeting your families at the Christmas party, not at the hospital." – Anthony Butcher*

Principle 4. Make data-based decisions

Safety culture has traditionally been highly focused on 'lagging' indicators, most notably TRIFR – 'total recordable incident frequency rate' – or days without a lost-time injury (LTI). These and related measures focus on rates of physical injury and of incidents, which are obviously important. They are also popular because they provide simple, numerical KPIs that are reportable and trackable over time.

However, these measures are prone to manipulation, most notably under-reporting. They also only tell part of the story. They are, as Rod Maule, General Manager of Safety and Wellbeing at Australia Post succinctly says, *"narrow, blunt instruments."* They look past social and psychological harm and in doing so overlook the most important factor – the people factor. As safety strategist David Pope puts it:

"People not getting hurt [has been] the outcome and therefore the measure. But I think we need to look at the success factors that

contribute to a safety culture that supports people to go home safe. It's certainly about our frontline leaders being able to understand their teams. We can look at the physics of how people can get hurt, and put controls in place, but you've also got to understand the people, how they make decisions, and the influence of their leadership and the people around them. And so, the success factors we measure need to tap into that element."

Safety practitioners we have worked with universally dislike TRIFR as a safety measuring KPI.

"Success has got to be bigger than numbers. It's got to be linked to people feeling comfortable with what they do and who they are and where they fit into the organisation. It's got to be linked to where we're sitting against those three things – the physical, social, and psychological experience of work… We've got to measure those things that actually get people to the place where they can thrive. And they're not going to thrive if they're worried about a hand being chopped off. And they're not going to thrive if they've been bullied. They're not going to thrive if they're having to work 15 hours every day." – Dr Kirstine Hulse

"We've ingrained these metrics [like TRIFR] and this way of thinking, and leaders feel safe and secure with them, even though there's so much research to say that you shouldn't. Those are terrible indicators! They don't actually predict anything, or give you any real trends, but we've created this safe feeling around them so it's really hard to actually shift away from that thinking or that level of control." – Bennjamin Mathews

"It certainly isn't enough to look at lost-time injuries and those sorts of lag indicators. Whilst they're good indicators, they're not entirely helpful, particularly when you're trying to look at a positive safety approach." – David Savio

"KPIs have potential to reinforce wrong behaviours by leaders, by Boards and by individuals; that's something important and in my opinion something we need to unlearn. The mentality is that if you get rewarded for not having an event, then you're going to hide it when someone does have an incident. Say we're over 200 days without an LTI, and though I'm an engineer and scientist, I'm superstitious about this. So, we don't talk about it - because that might jinx it."
– Linda Murry

The challenge is to identify safety measures that are leading indicators and provide sufficient data to make evidence-based decisions. If the data isn't telling you what you need to know, identify new, more suitable data that matches your strategic objectives. Seek to understand external factors that impact your people.

"We have learnt to be comfortable looking at other indicators; those that are more situational based and important at a local level. For instance, what the leader might be noticing in the workplace in terms of how people are performing, and whether that's aligning to the objective that they set for the day. It's no different to a coach, who would be observing the players in a game. They'll notice when a player isn't quite on plan, and so they'll make decisions [on that basis], and this might affect other players or the environment or alter the game plan, so they can support that player to get the best out of themselves." – David Savio

"We now track a whole heap of leading indicators. At a superinten-dent level, it's getting out into the field and getting your field time in. It's doing critical risk verifications to ensure that controls are in place. It's the quality of the investigations we undertake. It's looking at whether an investigation's actions have been completed and im-provement suggestions have been followed up. It's the coaching-based, peer-to-peer learning rituals. It's all of those things." – Craig Wise

"What does good look like? It's about how many times someone stops a job. It's about how many hazards have been reported and how many safety improvements we have done. Shifting the focus away from recordable incidents and onto these behaviours that are forward-looking lead indicators, rather than lag indicators." – Linda Murry

"I don't report on TRIFR or numbers of injuries. I don't measure TFRIF anymore. I highlight the high potential incidents based around risk level and risk potential, the number of controls that were still in place and frequency that it occurs rather than the actual injury level. [Measuring safety success is a] conversation I've had so many times with my wider team. We have this conversation almost every time we have our safety forums, in order to recalibrate. And I've had this conversation with the board and the exec team." – Dr Kirstine Hulse

"When we try and replace [TRIFR], it is really hard. For instance, if we decide to measure engagement, the board and others ask how robust that is. It's challenging. And I recognise that injury rates are a significant factor we need to consider. At Australia Post, 70% of the stuff that contributes to our workers' compensation provision are injuries that probably won't kill you.

"Then we have other risks that are rare but could potentially cause a fatality. These things very rarely contribute to our TRIFR, but they do contribute to our fatality risk. So, you need both. We need to monitor and report on our injury rates and fatality risks, as well as under-standing the culture and felt experience of the workforce." – Rod Maule

"Leading indicators and metrics that are more qualitative are quite hard to measure and to put a score on or a frequency rate. It can be challenging to influence the thinking around safety metrics and

success measures within large organisations. What I've been trying to do is just focus on the micro level, in a certain store and zone, and demonstrate change. And hopefully that has a ripple effect."
– Bennjamin Mathews

"We've been doing a lot of work around leading indicators. It's difficult, as you can imagine, because there's so many different types of indicators that you can use, some of them more subjective than others. So, we're playing around trying to find the right formula… I think for me, and I can also speak for the CEO, the success is more about stories, going out onto the farms and feeling a really good vibe among the team, and actually seeing a new person, who we've never seen report before, reporting an incident. When you see that there's banter, they're supporting each other and making good safety decisions… that's more of a success to me than LTI data." – Robyn Heap

Focus on leading indicators was also an area of emphasis in the work of Andrew Hopkins.[24]

"When an industry or an organisation is focused on identifying the early warnings signs of future catastrophes, the encouragement of incident reporting is critical. The objective is not necessarily to drive up the reporting of injuries, but to drive up the reporting of events that highlight when certain hazards are not adequately under control. In other words, to identify ineffective controls."

Hopkins also emphasises the importance of the quality of reports, not the quantity, and acknowledges the fact that it is a real challenge to ensure people do report. Central to this objective is a good reporting culture. The Brady Report points to the distorting factors associated with simple measurement of lost time injuries, for the reasons we have already highlighted, including underreporting, and the preferred focus on 'serious accident frequency rate' as a safety indicator.

---

24 Hopkins, A., 2009, *Learning from High Reliability Organisations*, Sydney, CCH Australia Ltd

"[Serious accident frequency rate] is considerably less susceptible to the quality of the industry's reporting culture and is therefore a better measure of level of safety in the industry. A positive safety culture is first and foremost a reporting culture. Therefore, the honest and accurate reporting of high potential incidents by the wider industry, and the encouragement to do so, should be of paramount importance."

Someone with extensive knowledge and experience in this area is Warren Smith, founder of critical risk management experts Incident Analytics. He cautions employers to make sure their 'deep-dive' investigations are focused on the right incidents, that is, on incidents with high serious injury or fatal outcome potential.

"Over the past ten years, our research has unveiled a concerning trend: about one in five recordable incidents have the potential for serious or fatal outcomes. Many of these events tend to fly under the radar due to a focus on 'actual' outcomes rather than 'potential' outcomes, leading to oversight of near miss events that could turn fatal. The opposite problem also exists for organisations that are investing too much in 'deep-dive' investigations for events with low or no high-severity potential. These two system phenomena combine to place the organisation at a learning disadvantage.

"One of the main reasons for this tendency to focus on the wrong incidents is the reliance on subjective judgment to determine severity potential. We recommend a shift, suggesting that organisations prioritise deep-dive investigations for events with predictable serious consequence potential. Once identified, we need to understand which risk controls failed, why they failed, and what can be done to strengthen control in future.

"We understand that there are individual and organisational factors underlying the incidents that occur. We first need to delve into the human error involved that allowed exposure to get out of control. This includes exploring cognitive hazards, skill issues and operating culture factors that may contribute. Secondly, we must analyse the

upstream systems and cultural factors that perpetuate weaknesses in risk control. This involves looking at organisational management systems and determining if they have an underlying role in these incidents."

Smith offers the example of a mining organisation his company worked with after they experienced near-fatal incidents. Incident Analytics conducted a 'Meta Incident Analysis' in 2021.

"The study of 168 incidents revealed that, besides operator slips, several upstream causal factors were significant contributors. Issues associated with local operational leadership, such as outdated procedures and a lack of follow-up, emerged as dominant outcomes. These factors were often missed in individual investigations, highlighting the need for a more comprehensive approach. In that case, we recognised that inconsistent leadership behaviour and addressing supervision capacity and competence in areas like job planning and high-risk task observation were crucial steps to reducing their high potential incidents."

Smith concludes that organisations can significantly improve their safety effectiveness by using the right data to understand the patterns of failure more accurately and then thoroughly implementing targeted actions.

Principle 5. Be curious

Consistent with the notion of adopting broader and more creative measurements of safety performance is a philosophy of encouraging curiosity. Nurturing a culture in which people feel supported to question the status quo, innovate and try new things without the risk of social harm plays an important role in safety culture maturity. Rewarding and encouraging leaders who ask questions and seek to truly understand, actively seek feedback – including 'bad news' – and always 'playing the ball, not the person', are central here. Investigation processes that focus on seeking to understand, not place blame, are other characteristics.

The need for curiosity applies equally to management. This can start with simply making it part of your routine to get out of the office and into the workplace on a regular basis, listening to the people who are doing the work, at their place of work. As we have seen, at Queensland Alumina they take this a step further, by making time spent in the field by superintendents and managers a leading indicator of their safety culture.

Dr Kirstine Hulse tells a vivid story that illustrates the power of curiosity and the power of getting out on the floor.

> "For a few years I lived and worked in South Africa. On my first day, one thing stood out that changed my approach as a leader. I was in a technical role as a process superintendent in an aluminium smelter. On this first day, I thought I'd take the production supervisor, Thando, and the maintenance supervisor, Arno, out on the floor together with me.

> "Aluminium smelters are enormous, and you have to walk for ages to get across the plant. I met the two men at our office to walk together and just after we set out towards the plant, we arrived at this double door. Thando got there first, opened the door, and went through ahead of us, after which Arno pulled his side of the door open and gestured for me to go through. Then the two proceeded to argue over who should go through the door first, both taking very different stances. Meanwhile, I'm thinking about how I'm also capable of opening the door. I hadn't anticipated that this would be our first problem to resolve.

> "After finally negotiating the door and as we continued on our way, I learnt from Thando that in his culture, a man goes through the door first. From Arno's perspective and culture, opening the door for a woman was just as deeply ingrained.

> "So, in the simple act of going through a door, it turned out that we had three completely different and well-ingrained cultural norms at

play. And the thing was that we were all correct. You can have polar opposite viewpoints, and still be right. It was quite an eye-opener that something so simple could be so complicated. Do you automate the door? Do you meet on the other side of the door, or do you negotiate it each time? Do you have to go with what feels familiar?

"The important thing that came out of this was the recognition that it is okay to have completely opposite opinions or perspectives, and it doesn't necessarily mean that one of you is wrong. You can both be right while disagreeing, but it is important to seek understanding. It's a different type of thinking for leaders to understand that, for people to have self-awareness and to be curious and open-minded and interested in learning more about different opinions or perspectives."

David Pope described an experience he had while working at a refinery that provided a similarly powerful lesson.

"It was during the annual maintenance shutdown and there were two identical pump sets being worked on – very large pumps. Johno was the frontline leader of his team, 15A, and Peter was the leader of 15B. We had 1,000 people doing work on the shutdown, and safety is always an issue because you have all these extra contractors off the street, which means you can't always control the quality of those workers. It was a challenge just to get them all inducted and ensure they weren't going to hurt themselves in this environment.

"Now, both Johno and Peter were overseeing the same type of work on their two teams. There's nothing particularly unusual about that, except that an injury occurred on Johno's team: old mate Clifton hurt his back on the very first day of a ten-day overhaul project. This got me wondering, 'What's going on here?' so we carried out an in-vestigation. It was soon obvious that Johno didn't have his worksite organised. He hadn't organised permits and the area looked messy. Meanwhile, to my right, only about 50 metres away, I could see Peter and his team working on their very similar job, but in their case,

the work area was clearly well planned and well organised. Visiting them, I found that all the permits were in place and that their people were communicating well and working well together.

"*On the second day, there was another incident with Johno's crew. Then on the third day, I turned up just before smoko break, to find that the 15A crew had already left for their break, while Peter's team was still working. A little while later, we got into our project review and planning, and we found that 15A was way behind, while 15B was way ahead. I visited Peter's group again and, of course, they were still well organised, methodically working through the task, travelling pretty easily. On the other work site, it was still a mess, and the talk was all complaints of, 'We ain't got this,' 'We ain't got that,' 'We're always struggling,' and 'Johno's always off somewhere else!'*

"*In the end, we actually had an interesting opportunity to experiment. Johno, unfortunately, had to take some time off for personal reasons. We had another guy, Steve, who would fill in for him, but we decided that rather than have Steve fill in on 15A, we would see what happened if we moved Peter to 15A from 15B. Steve would continue running the ship that was already working well.*

"*And guess what happened to the 15A crew? Same people, same job, same status... but a different supervisor. Things turned around in no time. This experience was – bam! – the importance of great frontline leaders came through loud and clear. They are the ones who build strong foundations; they are the ones who hunt for the good stuff; they are the ones who actively care and know and understand what's going on with their teams. Not the CEO, not the refinery manager who came out to walk around the shutdown, you know, once every two weeks, and it would be the 'ducks on the pond' effect where they'd all vanish. It's your frontline leaders who have the strongest influence over the team.*"

Aside from the obvious message here about the importance of excellent frontline leaders, management in this instance needed to have enough curiosity to run their 'experiment'. The easy path would have been to leave Peter in place – "If it ain't broke, don't fix it." But making the switch provided them with valuable insight that they could carry forward as they worked to build a more positive safety culture.

Another element of what we're calling curiosity relates to authenticity in seeking the truth. This is particularly the case when it comes to the way incident investigations are carried out. David explains:

"In my experience, particularly in mining and heavy industry, something that drives a certain behaviour is investigation method-ologies. This is not a dig at anyone, but I think a lot of investigations' methodologies came back to a human factor. Regardless of the type, these investigations are all relatively similar, because the decision trees are almost identical, and this often drives the wrong focus. Rather than trying to look at how we make the workplace a safe place to be, in too many investigations we don't always get the full facts because people don't feel safe when making their statements. Therefore, when you've got to work out what really occurred, the decision trees drove us down a certain avenue that is geared around forcing people to fit the box."

We have seen this ourselves on a number of occasions. The intent of incident investigations is to try and learn, in order to make things safer in the future. However, the way that investigations are conducted can have a marked impact on a worker's feeling of psychological safety and their social connection with their leaders and their peers. This can affect the quality of data that you collect, which in turn affects your ability to improve physical safety.

Real curiosity means authentically teasing out the facts in order to make meaningful improvements. That requires curiosity about the effectiveness of investigation procedures in the first place.

Professor Andrew Hopkins[25] describes organisations in which leaders use curiosity to unveil the possibility of failure as mindful, 'high reliability' organisations.

> *"Mindfulness is not just a characteristic of organisations. It is also a characteristic of their leaders. Mindful leaders are very aware that their systems may not be working as well as intended, nor as well as they are being told by their subordinates. They are suspicious of a steady stream of good news and are forever probing for the bad news that they know lies beneath the surface. Mindful leaders therefore conduct regular walk-arounds, talking to employees on site, seeking the view from the frontline. They know there is no point telling people that safety is the top priority. That is likely to be seen as no more than a slogan. Instead, they approach workers with a degree of humility – humble inquiry[26] – seeking to learn from them what is going wrong and what the organisation could do better."*

Finally, curiosity needs to extend to the very top of the organisation.

> *"A principle-led safety culture has to start at the CEO. The ability to make sound, data-based decisions can be limited by the impact of over-bearing CEOs who hold a biased mindset around data. Approaching data and looking at data in an unbiased way is such a key, important aspect. And that links to being curious and open minded. I have seen what happens when a change in leadership brings in a CEO who knows they don't know everything, and they lead with curiosity. This new CEO started asking, 'What is that? Where's the data to support that?' And suddenly we had a data-driven decision-making process. Having key leaders being curious, being open minded, wanting to question the data. That's what supports safety."* – David Pope

---

25 Hopkins, A. (2021). A practical guide to becoming a "High Reliability Organisation."

26 Schein, E. (2013). Humble Inquiry: The Gentle Art of Asking Instead of Telling, Berrett-Koehler Publishers, San Francisco.

Principle 6. Keep it simple

Keeping messaging simple and aligned with the goal of positive safety is an effective way to avoid 'losing' people in a fog of compliance. Focusing on the critical risks that can cause life-changing injuries, then beyond that, creating freedom within a framework are two of the simplest areas to pay attention to. Solve safety challenges rather than relying on administrative actions and piling on more rules. This can be done in many areas in both training and process.

Working at a site within the giant BHP multinational, as with any corporation, can have its challenges when it comes to keeping things simple. For Linda Murry, there have been efforts to adapt corporate training to make it more relevant in the Hay Point context.

"BHP as a whole has taken every single employee and contractor through 'active bystander' training. This is very much in response to the Australian Human Rights Commission's Respect@Work report around sexual assault and sexual harassment in the workplace. We felt that the standard training wasn't really written with frontline workers in mind, so we modified it to make it real, putting realistic examples in it and condensing it down to a manageable timeframe. We made it relevant for them and created that emotional connection by asking, 'Have you got a mother, have you got a grandmother, have you got a daughter?' When we keep the message simple and make it realistic for them, the training can be highly successful."

At Kmart, Bennjamin Mathews is leading an effort to simplify incident reporting.

"At Kmart, only staff leaders in the store can report incidents. If a team member has an incident or near miss, they don't actually have access to the system to report it. They have to verbally do that through a leader. We feel like that's a barrier. It impedes open and honest reporting, particularly if some of the issues are with the

leaders themselves... That could increase underreporting or reduce the quality of reporting, so we want to remove that barrier. We're focusing on creating a new reporting system that improves the user experience for reporting incidents. It will involve training and education around changing the language, so instead of 'investigations', they will be 'learning events'. And we want to have different methods for investigation to ensure that when things do go wrong, our first point isn't blame. It's about understanding the situation and then looking at where the accountability sits."

The Brady Report pointed to a source of frustration for a great many people in safety management: excessive, complex paperwork. A significant proportion of people spoken to during the review brought up the challenge of producing and managing a large amount of paperwork, usually associated with an increasing number of safety procedures.

While all accept some paperwork is required – at least to establish compliance – they were of the view that the sheer quantity of it resulted in them spending more time at their desks than actively in the field talking to and observing the workers. In their view – consistent with the experience at Queensland Alumina – the importance of spending time on the mine site or underground was critical, both in identifying hazards and ensuring work was being carried out in line with procedures. Not having time to do this, they felt, was a very high price to pay in order to keep on top of their paperwork, and could very well be leading to a point where the bureaucracy was effectively making a site *less* safe.

To many, this ever-increasing paperwork load came in the form of more and more procedures. Many felt this was the default approach to managing risk.

Principle 7. Hunt the good stuff

How? By concentrating on the presence of safety, not just the absence of harm. By focusing on the potential of your people, supporting them to adapt, learn, and be resourceful. By building trust, acknowledging their expertise at what they do and seeking their input when searching for solutions. By seeing your people as an army of problem solvers, not an army of problems. These are all examples of seeking out and acknowledging the positive, which sets in motion a beneficial cycle of ever more positive safety. Sometimes this takes some effort, but shifting your focus away from reducing negative behaviour and towards reinforcing positive behaviour is always worth it. As Craig Wise said:

> "When our leaders spend time every day on site, connecting with the team members, they are there to look for and give recognition for great work – they are there to hunt the good stuff."

Wise reflected on a leadership ritual they instigated, which was focused on building relationships with the team, with leaders seeking to understand the work being done and the support the team needs. Finding and recognising positive attitudes, decision making and behaviours in their team members has enabled them to really turn the perception of safety leaders around. As Craig explains:

> "After these walks [around the plant], the whole team comes back together and the person who led the interaction reflects on what went well, what the opportunities are for improvement and how impactful it was for the team members. Then the coach who observed the interaction gives their feedback on what they saw, again recognising what was done well, as well as things that can be improved. As our maturity as an organisation has improved, we are seeing this as a way to hold each other accountable at a very high level. We've found that because we do hunt the good stuff and reflect on each other's strengths and give recognition where it's due, it has given us the ability for leaders to challenge each other in good faith and give honest, constructive feedback."

At Australia Post, part of hunting the good stuff means looking beyond overly simple, one-dimensional reward structures and instead instigating rewards that reveal leaders who can build and support a citizenship culture.

> *"Part of creating a positive safety culture is about reward structures. In Australia Post, if we rewarded people for productivity measures – a good postie who always gets the job done, rain, hail, or shine, or a good supervisor of posties who makes sure the posties get the job done, rain, hail, or shine – if we were then to say safety is really important, the likely response would be, 'Well, is it?' You've got to recognise that this needs to change. We need to shift the focus of our reward and recognitions framework from promoting based on pro-ductivity measures alone to promoting people for productivity and safety and engagement. Being the least productive but most engaged leader is not ideal and nor is being the most productive leader who's really disengaged and hard to work with. People won't put up with the overbearing, production-at-all-costs style of leadership anymore. I don't think they ever responded well to it – they just put up with it in the old days – but they certainly don't tolerate it now. You've got to engage with people and be a decent human being. So, to drive a positive culture, you need to have some structures and rewards for being a decent human – being a collaborative, supportive leader who creates a physically and socially and psychologically safe team envi-ronment."* – Rod Maule

Professor Hopkins[27] highlights some brilliant cases to demonstrate that in order to create a culture of fearless reporting, organisations must hunt the good stuff by celebrating the reporting of hazards and near misses.

> *"To encourage the reporting of bad news, organisations must celebrate particularly significant reports. There is a famous case where a seaman on an aircraft carrier thought he might have left a tool on the deck. Foreign objects on a runway are very dangerous. Accordingly,*

---

27 Ibid, Hopkins 2021

the seaman reported the loss of the tool to the commanding officer of the carrier. There were aircraft in the sky at the time that had to be diverted to a shore base. The tool was found and the aircraft brought back on board. The whole episode involved a substantial disruption to the activities of the aircraft carrier. The next day the commander summoned the crew to the deck and held a ceremony in which he congratulated the seaman for having made the report."

Hopkins points out that financial rewards also have a place in this kind of recognition. He describes one leader who introduced an award to encourage the reporting of bad news in her organisation. The reward was named after someone in the organisation who had saved someone's life by doing just that.

"The award had various levels, the highest being diamond, which was worth $1,000. The day I visited her she made a diamond award to an operator who had recognised that an alarm level had been changed on a piece of equipment, without going through the proper management of change process. He had written an email about this to his manager, who in turn had passed it up the line. The senior manager I was visiting had made more than a hundred awards for this kind of vital reporting in a period of less than 12 months."

Principle 8. Make an impact

Having an 'impact' in a positive safety culture means so much more than zero harm. The real impact comes when the culture changes, not only in safety but across the board. This can include focusing on the whole person with health and wellbeing initiatives, actively promoting diversity and inclusion and embracing positive workplace behaviours. Being a great place to work with a welcoming and high-trust culture is very rewarding. This is where lasting impact can be found.

"It's an 11-hour drive for me to [Lawson Grains'] most northern farm. But we work hard to create a psychologically safe working environment in which people have the confidence to put their hands up and report near misses and incidents without the fear of blame. For us, being face to face and speaking directly to every single employee has huge benefits. It can be challenging to do that, of course. It takes a whole week for the executive just to meet with people over in WA. That's why we work on showing care and empathy and keeping that consistent messaging that you're not going to get blasted for raising concerns or reporting an incident. I tell the group how it affects us when we open a 'new incident' report and we have that moment of fear that one of our people is significantly hurt, because we value them as people first and employees second.

"We get everyone together once a year in March for our annual conference and then all the farm managers in August. These get togethers are about connecting, building relationships, learning, and discussing the important things. We make sure that we factor in a two to four hour session where it's an open book, where the CEO and executive team will listen to all the questions, challenges, and concerns of our people. Sometimes they'll work together, collectively, on a certain concern, working through it, and talking it out. This is one way we aim to create a high-trust environment and ensure our workplace is an environment where people truly feel heard, valued, and respected. The best part is seeing the benefits of this investment in our culture flowing both ways. Our 'People and Wellbeing First' values have a positive impact on our teams, and they, in turn, pass that culture on to our new employees. We have found that teams living this culture motivate those around them to operate at the same level. This is important to us, particularly because some of our teams are far away from our head office in fairly remote areas." – Robyn Heap

Agriculture, and family farms in particular, have long contributed disproportionately to rates of workplace injury and death. Lawson Grains has been able to extend its impact beyond its own properties' fences through the work they do with their own employees.

"We know that in agriculture [generally], we've still got a long way to go with regards to safety and wellbeing. So, in improving our own safety culture, we're also trying to lift our neighbours and the communities that we live in and work in and [across] the whole industry. When we put on new employees, [many of them will] be coming from a family farm, so then we're starting from scratch again [with improving their approach to safety]. Compared to mining, where they're usually putting on experienced miners who are already at a high level in terms of safety, our people are likely to be coming from a really low base. The good news is that when people leave and go back out, they take with them the knowledge and experience of working safely and having a positive mindset." – Robyn Heap

Linda Murry values the impact she is able to contribute to by working with a large multinational firm.

"We are not an NGO. I work for a multinational and our job is to not only bring people and resources together to build a better world, but it's also to make sure shareholders' expectations are met. You can do that in a respectful way that has a lot of positive impact. That's part of the reason why I've stayed with big multinationals. I have the ability to do a lot of philanthropic work that I would not be able to do otherwise. We've given away houses to domestic violence shelters, and we've been able to donate money to the local soccer club and to community projects, etc. The social impact we have is incredibly important to us."

For Sentis, the aim is to make a tangible impact on the environment through our Banyula Conservation Reserve. Managing Director and Banyula Conservation Reserve Founder Tony O'Brien shares what inspired him to establish the reserve.

"The inspiration for Banyula goes hand in hand with Sentis's broader commitment to changing people and communities for the better. In 2019, we witnessed the devastating fires that swept through our local area, and it was a wakeup call. We realised that as a company, we have the resources and the responsibility to contribute to the restoration of our natural heritage. Banyula is more than just a conservation reserve; it's our commitment to sustainability, environmental preservation, and leaving a positive legacy for future generations.

"The expansion of Banyula in 2021 allowed us to broaden our impact, both ecologically and in terms of community involvement. With an additional 332 hectares, we can do more in terms of biodiversity preservation, implementing innovative conservation strategies, and engaging the local community in meaningful ways. It aligns with Sentis's mission to create a lasting, positive impact on the environment and the communities we serve.

"We believe science is at the heart of meaningful conservation efforts. The wildlife monitoring program, plant and bird species identification, and the feasibility study for a predator-proof enclosure are all crucial components of our strategy. By employing a science-based approach, we're not just making well-intentioned efforts; we're making informed decisions that have a real impact. It ensures that our conservation work is effective, sustainable, and contributes to the broader field of environmental science.

"Celebrating 20 years at Sentis is a momentous occasion, but for me, it's not just about looking back; it's about the ongoing journey. Banyula represents the spirit of adventure and the commitment to doing something meaningful. We recognise that we have a unique opportunity to make a difference, not only in the corporate world but in the broader context of environmental conservation. It's about innovation, positive impact, and ensuring that our business leaves the world in a better place than we found it."

7.
THE SAFETY LEADER'S PLAYBOOK

"Knowledge is of no value unless you put it into practice."

~Anton Chekhov

By this point in this book, we have hopefully made a convincing argument that positive safety and a safe, well and engaged workforce are things worth aspiring to, with benefits that represent substantial improvements over more traditional approaches to safety. As can be seen in the contrast between the Lawson Grains story and Julie's story in Chapter 3, these benefits extend far beyond safety.

In Chapter 4, we introduced the concept of the Safety Culture Maturity Model, with safety citizenship representing the gold standard of safety culture. However, our research has shown that safety cultures with this level of maturity are extremely rare. In fact, in our 2019 study, not one of the 73 sites we surveyed met the criteria. We rated only two of those sites as having a safety culture operating at the collaborative level, meaning that only those two sites in our study displayed a truly positive culture.

You may be thinking that this indicates we've set the bar too high – that surely more sites could be given a higher rating if we were just a bit more realistic. We beg to differ. In truth, the single biggest difference between these two sites and the rest was the degree of cooperation on safety matters between the workers themselves and between workers and management.

Put simply, on these sites, safety is much more than a one-dimensional focus on the absence of harm. Instead, the focus is on the *presence* of safety. Safety is three-dimensional, addressing the physical, social, and psychological experiences of everyone. Responsibility for safety is authentically shared. Everyone looks out for each other; everyone believes that they and their workmates, at all levels, have the right to be and feel safe at work, physically, psychologically, and socially, all the time. No one sees keeping themselves or others safe as a chore.

But positive safety is even more than that. In a positive, mature safety environment, leaders and their people feel competent, confident, and grounded. They have the physical and mental capacity to do their jobs. Visitors to the plant or office are struck by the relative calm that pervades the place. People are engaged, connected to the purpose of their work, and intrinsically motivated. They know they are making a contribution. They are challenged, but they have the skills, resources, and motivation to meet the challenge.

In other words, the workforce is *safe, well* and *engaged.*

Is that too much to ask? Is it unrealistic?

It may seem like an ideal – and a long way off – however, our experience is that when leaders truly commit themselves to achieving positive safety, it can be done – even in the most challenging environments. Reaching safety citizenship won't happen overnight, but the first steps can be taken quickly and will immediately make a difference.

In this chapter we want to provide some thoughts on those things you, as a leader, need to prioritise in order to shift your organisation's safety culture to a higher level of maturity from where you are now – and then to a higher level again.

We won't be prescriptive: every organisation is different. And yes, you need to be pragmatic: for cultural change to be successful, executive alignment and commitment both in principle and in practice are fundamental. This means a commitment of more than just budget. It means committing time and effort to the journey. Cultures can take years to turn around. This won't be achieved with one-off safety training or changes to the incentive program.

But we can provide guidance on how to use your influence to drive change, along with providing some practical tools and strategies to get you started. In helping you plan your way forward, we'll be referring back to three of the models we've introduced you to:

- The ABR model (attitude, behaviour and results – Chapter 5)
- The Safety Culture Model (SCM – Chapter 3)
- The concept of three-dimensional safety experience (Chapter 4)
- The eight principles of positive safety (Chapter 6)

We'll also draw on our exploration of the brain's response to change and our understanding of the brain's role in keeping us and others safe (Chapter 5).

Jobs to be done at the board and CEO level

Focus point 1: Change comes from the top

The last two decades of the 20th century were the peak of the 'greed is good' profit-at-all-costs era. CEOs like Jack Welch at GE and 'Chainsaw Al' Albert Dunlap at Sunbeam made celebrities of themselves by creating huge profits with substantial help from cost cutting. Much as they still are today, a newly appointed CEO was expected to talk up the share price, emphasising margins, profitability, and shareholder returns.

But there was one CEO who took a very different approach. After Paul O'Neill was appointed to the top job at Alcoa in the US, he stepped in front of his first shareholder meeting and talked about safety. *"I intend to make Alcoa the safest company in America,"* he is quoted as saying. *"I intend to go for zero injuries."* He didn't mention cost cutting or profits or market domination, so, perhaps needless to say, his message was not what investors and brokers wanted to hear. Many sold off their Alcoa stock immediately after the meeting.

Undaunted, O'Neill then set the company on a single-minded path to improve its safety record. There was no escape. After any injury, plant managers were required to advise O'Neill himself, within 24 hours, of their plan to avoid the same thing happening again. That meant they needed to instigate effective systems within their plants so that the news of any injury was reported to them in a very short time.

O'Neill encouraged everyone, at every level, to look out for safety hazards, report them and act on them. He even gave his personal number to workers, urging them to call him at home if their managers didn't follow through on improvements.

What O'Neill understood and his investors did not, was that a wholesale focus on safety would force the rest of the business to realign itself as well. *"If we bring our injury rates down, it will be because the individuals at this company have agreed to become part of something important: they've devoted themselves to creating a habit of excellence. Safety will be an indicator that we're making progress in changing our habits across the whole institution."*

O'Neill was like a physiotherapist who solves a patient's back pain by having them exercise more, not less, because he understood that everything is connected to everything else. Like the physio, he also knew that his patient would need constant reminding to do those exercises until a new habit formed.

O'Neill's unrelenting focus on safety worked. Without mentioning profit-ability as a target, it came anyway, as safety system improvements cascaded into improvements in other areas and the business grew more and more efficient. By the time O'Neill retired in 2000, the company's revenue was five times higher than when he had started, as was its share price. Plus, it was one of the safest companies in the world.

The Alcoa story reminds us of two things. First, that improving safety can have beneficial knock-on effects on the rest of an organisation. Second, and perhaps more importantly, that if you really want to change a culture, that change needs to be driven from the very top of the organisation. If the board and its CEO are not authentically behind the change, if they're not willing to live the change, it is much less likely to stick. That is as true of building a positive safety culture as it is of any other change. Culture starts at the top, so that's where the buy-in needs to start.

We can contrast the O'Neill story with that of another CEO: BP's Tony Hayward. In 2010, an explosion on the BP-operated Deepwater Horizon offshore oil drilling platform led to a disaster that killed 11 crew and caused the largest marine oil spill in history, with massive social and economic impacts on the Gulf of Mexico. The catastrophe resulted in billions of dollars in losses to the company. This incident was substantially contrib-uted to by attitudes that contradicted good safety practices.

At the time, the project was running massively over budget and there was a strong drive from management to finish up and get out of there, even if that meant cutting corners. When the safest action would have been to take more time and spend more money addressing a multitude of untended maintenance issues, decisions were made to keep pushing on and 'just get the job done'. According to one analysis,[28] language used in speeches by Hayward "*contributed rhetorically to an ideology of economic efficiency and cost control, in a manner that was inconsistent with an enduring safety culture.*"

---

28 Amernic, J., & Craig, R. (2017). CEO speeches and safety culture: British Petroleum before the Deepwater Horizon Disaster. https://www.sciencedirect.com/science/article/abs/pii/S1045235416300740

In our work with clients, particularly those in large companies with many layers of leadership and complex organisational structures involving multiple sites, we have seen time and again how crucial it is for safety culture to be driven from the top.

However, health and safety management is often regarded as a support role – not as something that deserves the board's close attention. At board level in particular, there is a tendency to see safety as a management issue, not a strategic issue. When this attitude is also adopted by the CEO, it often cascades down through the rest of the organisation.

The outcome is a belief that profit comes first and that of course safety is important... when it doesn't compromise profitability. When that happens, the organisation's safety culture defaults to a focus on compliance. It becomes all about zero harm and nothing more, because everyone will know that reporting zero harm is the best way to remove safety as a potential source of the board's attention. That number alone will tick the safety box.

Not only does board-level ambivalence about safety ultimately threaten employees' wellbeing, but it also ignores the role of safety in achieving the very thing that board exists to achieve: sustainable business success. The widely understood purpose of the board as head of an organisation, in partnership with its CEO, is to provide strategic oversight, ensure accountability and make key decisions that guide the organisation's direction and future.

This includes ensuring the organisation's financial health, ethical operations, and compliance with laws and regulations, while also representing the interests of stakeholders. Even if, as typically happens, health and safety appear on the board's agenda only in the context of ensuring legal compliance and avoiding litigation, it still makes safety a board-level issue. Those governing an organisation ultimately have to invest in safety in order to protect the organisation from negative financial, ethical, or reputational consequences.

Put simply, building a safety culture helps avoid bad stuff happening. As the Australian Institute of Company Directors puts it:

"Effective governance identifies culture as an important lever to create value. Organisations with a stronger, positive culture may not only face lower risk (for example, from misconduct) but may also exhibit greater resilience overall, higher customer satisfaction, better employee morale and wellbeing, and enhanced productivity and performance against strategy over the long term."[29]

While ensuring compliance and legal protections are obviously essential responsibilities, the board's interest in safety doesn't need to stop there. As the Paul O'Neill example demonstrates, driving a consistently positive safety culture can actually be a catalyst for the achievement of positive results in all areas of a business.

To reiterate a point made a number of times in this book, a compliance culture emphasises the absence of harm, but stopping at compliance leaves on the table the enormous potential of positive safety, including levels of engagement, discretionary effort and trust that will have flow-on effects to all other areas. When people look out for one another and contribute to the improvement of their organisation out of genuine care for the people and place to which they feel they belong, all stakeholders benefit.

It takes bold and forward-thinking leadership to move beyond the safety cultures of public and private compliance and towards the loftier and more impactful target of safety citizenship. However, safety messages that come from the highest levels of the business, are connected to the values of the organisation, and provide a vision of what we want to see, when communicated with passion and genuine care, are immensely inspiring. The Paul O'Neill story is a case in point. These messages can galvanise the hearts and minds of the people toward a shared goal and create the desire to work toward them out of a sense of pride and self-identity.

---

29 *Governing Organisational Culture*, Australian Institute of Company Directors

Focus point 2: Provide clarity and set the priorities

In early 2013, an investigation publicly revealed that a group of male members of the Australian Army had produced highly inappropriate material demeaning women, which they then distributed on the internet. In a message to members of the army recorded in June 2013 and uploaded to YouTube, Chief of Army Lieutenant General David Morrison was unequivocal, saying there was "*no place*" in the army for members who "*exploit and demean*" their colleagues.

General Morrison's speech clearly framed the goal that the army has to be an inclusive organisation, in which every soldier, man or woman, is able to reach their full potential and is encouraged to do so. He pulled no punches in calling out the unacceptable behaviour and connected a shared responsibility for a respectful workplace with a sense of honour and duty. Here is an excerpt from General Morrison's speech:

> "*Every one of us is responsible for the culture and reputation of our army and the environment in which we work. If you become aware of any individual degrading another, then show moral courage, and take a stand against it.*

> "*I will be ruthless in ridding the army of people who cannot live up to its values. And I need every one of you to support me in achieving this. The standard you walk past is the standard you accept. That goes for all of us, but especially those who, by their rank, have a leadership role.*

> "*If we are a great national institution, if we care about the legacy left to us by those who have served before us, if we care about the legacy we leave to those who, in turn, will protect and secure Australia, then it is up to us to make a difference. If you're not up to it, find something else to do with your life. There is no place for you amongst this band of brothers and sisters.*"

This impassioned and impactful speech clearly establishes how this safety issue is connected to Australian Army values. It demonstrates leadership commitment right from the top, and it does so in a way that is clear and leaves no doubt about General Morrison's priorities. The speech was not about forcing change, but getting buy-in and having listeners want to improve respect and inclusiveness within the organisation because that's the sort of people they are – honourable men and women who want to feel proud of the legacy they leave behind.

In Chapter 4, we told the story of agricultural company Lawson Grains and its holistic approach to safety. Not mentioned in that initial story are the challenges Lawson Grains face in maintaining its vision for safety in an industry not known for having a strong safety culture.

The rates of physical injury and fatality in the agricultural industry are higher than other industries, recording 14.7 fatalities per 100,000 workers in 2022 in contrast to 9.5 in the transport, postal and warehousing industry, and a mere 2.4 in mining.[30] In large part, this is related to the fact that most people in the industry come from (or still work on) family farms.

It's a generalisation, but the nature of small farms means that safety often comes second or third behind 'just getting the job done' and keeping one's head above water financially. If you've spent half an hour driving your tractor out into a paddock and it breaks down, chances are you're going do whatever it takes to get it working – even if that means doing something you know is risky – rather than losing half a day's work walking back to the shed to fetch the right tools for the job.

The same applies to psychosocial risks like excessive working hours, fatigue, and the mental health challenges of dealing with too little rain when it's needed, too much rain at the wrong times, plagues of mice or locusts, fluctuations in grain prices… the list is endless. Again, the typical attitude of the family farmer is to stoically soldier on, largely because there is no realistic alternative.

30 Key Work Health and Safety Statistics Australia, 2023

These are all behaviours that Lawson Grains discourages. Putting aside the human cost, on a purely pragmatic level, if someone is hurt trying to avoid a productivity loss, the company endures productivity loss anyway, in addition to the cost of the injury. The same applies to ignored psychosocial harm.

Lawson Grains' attitude is that no machine should be operated if it isn't 100% safe, and if an extra worker is needed because people are working excessive hours, that person will be made available. This is obviously quite different thinking to the typical family farm. As a result, Lawson Grains' senior management personnel spend a lot of time and effort setting and communicating their priorities around safety, especially with new or casual employees who may have come off a family farm. They drive home the 'safety first' message with their farm managers, but also directly with employees, face to face, to ensure the message is heard with clarity.

The safety mission and vision of companies like Lawson Grains, or Alcoa in the previous example, establish a standard of excellence. They give individuals clarity on their priorities as they go about their day-to-day work. When team members are inspired and engaged by a vision, they know where they are going and what they need to do to get there. More importantly, they continue to work towards shared goals associated with the vision, even when their leader is not physically present. This ultimately leads to increased safety performance and a shift towards behaviours that reflect safety citizenship.

In our research, we defined safety mission and vision in terms of employee awareness of the organisation's safety vision and values, as well as their involvement in the development and integration of the mission and vision into daily activities. We found that a clear safety mission and vision was a top strength for 60% of those sites at private compliance and mateship levels, compared to those within the counterproductive and public compliance cultures.[31]

---

31 Access the Driving a Positive Safety Culture 2020 report from the List of Resources at the end of the book.

At these sites, workers reported that they not only understood the vision, but that they believed in it personally. This contrasts with companies that displayed negative safety cultures, in which the best workers reported that they were aware of the vision – not that they also believed in it. As such, both the quality of the vision and leaders' commitment to driving it throughout all levels of the business were key differentiators when comparing negative and positive safety cultures.

Characteristics of those sites that displayed strong a safety mission and vision included:

- a perceived genuine commitment to safety values from the organisation
- safety targets/goals/objectives that were clearly defined
- a safety vision that was seen as consistent and credible
- integration of the vision into regular processes such as toolbox talks and pre-start meetings
- commitment by leaders to driving the safety vision and communicating it consistently
- commitment to the vision at all levels of the business.

Creating and sharing a safety vision is one of the few competencies that is not required at the worker level. Rather, it is a unique skill required only of leaders. This creates an interesting challenge because as individuals rise through the ranks into positions of leadership, they can often struggle to demonstrate skill in this area, simply because they've never previously had to.

Let's be honest, developing and sharing an effective vision is no easy task. It takes time to plan, think and develop specific goals to create a vision and more effort to create the activities and words needed to get teams to engage with the vision and then to take positive steps towards achieving it. This can often result in leaders placing safety mission and vision in the 'too hard' basket with the demands of day-to-day activities all too often getting in the way of progress.

The sites we found that identified safety mission and vision as a strength had leaders at the forefront taking on the responsibility for communicating the vision to their teams and regularly driving it home. Leaders who are successful in this area are consistent in their messaging, communicate the vision with their teams on a regular basis, and invite their teams to contribute to the vision where possible.

Organisational leaders – from board level down – need to share responsibility for conveying and consistently reinforcing the safety vision, as well as building the skills more junior leaders need to develop. Given only 12% of leaders in our survey[32] felt confident that they were highly effective at sharing safety vision, this is clearly an area of leadership development that is frequently overlooked.

Organisations that invest in their leaders to develop their leadership skills also help to develop broader skills, creating positive effects in all areas of the business. But again, for this to happen effectively and sustainably, it needs support from the board and CEO.

Focus point 3: Be aware of the influence of your success measures

"You manage what you measure" is a truism as old as management itself. It is common, especially in larger businesses, for safety performance to be measured using only lagging indicators such as TRIFR and LTIFR. However, ultimately, measures such as this are not measuring *safety* in terms of avoidance of the risk of injury, the extent of those risks that exist, the drivers of those risks, nor the effectiveness of controls over them. All they really tell us, in hindsight, is how often the threat of an existing risk (whether previously known or not) was realised.

To reiterate a point quoted earlier from David Pope: *"You've also got to understand the people, how they make decisions, and the influence of their*

---

32   The State of Safety Leadership. Sentis (2017). Access the study in the List of Resources at the end of the book.

leadership and the people around them." The standard lagging indicators reveal none of this.

As we discussed in the section 'Make data-based decisions' in Chapter 6, these measures have their place in benchmarking, but our research has shown that if these are the only significant measures, they can lead to unintended behaviours: most noticeably, underreporting of near misses, incidents, and injuries.

In a review of the issues in measuring and reporting health and safety issues, Safe Work Australia found that of approximately 141,000 injured workers who received financial assistance from their employers between 2009-2010, 92,000 received regular sick leave rather than workers' compensation payments.[33] We have to presume that these 'sick days' were not recorded as lost time.

Notably, almost 31% of absences compensated through ordinary sick leave related to injuries requiring five or more days' absence from work. This seems consistent with anecdotal claims that individuals manipulate injury performance measures by underreporting lost-time injuries, though it may also be that employers encourage this approach to avoid initiating a workers' compensation case and subsequent damage to their insurance premiums.

Then there is the issue of mental stress and other psychosocial injuries, which have long had a stigma associated with them. The ABS work-related injuries survey of 2009-10 revealed that over 70% of workers who reported experiencing work-related mental stress did not apply for workers' compensation.[34]

One way to improve these measures would be to take the Paul O'Neill

---

33 Issues in the Measurement and Reporting of Work Health and Safety Performance: A Review (2013). Safe Work Australia.

34 Issues in the Measurement and Reporting of Work Health and Safety Performance: A Review. (2013). Safe Work Australia.

approach and insist on every single incident being reported directly to the CEO, but this is probably a bit drastic! In any case, it is still an after-the-fact indicator and not preventative.

A much more effective approach to safety success measures is tracking what we call positive safety performance metrics (PSPMs). The purpose of PSPMs is to provide data that can assess the presence of positive safety and reveal the deeper story in the data to understand what is really driving the safety outcomes and where improvement is needed, thus informing safety culture strategy more effectively.

These indicators aim to detect and provide advance warning of latent safety hazards and risks across the three dimensions of safety experience. This allows organisations to implement proactive actions designed to prevent future safety incidents. (PSPMs may also be lagging indicators while simultaneously providing forward looking insights.)

PSPMs can be tricky to manage (and thus potentially less attractive to senior management and boards) because each organisation's PSPMs will be unique, dependent on their unique safety issues and challenges. They are not, therefore, easy to benchmark across organisations.

Alumina refinery Queensland Alumina Limited (QAL), based in Gladstone, 500 kilometres north of Brisbane, provides some good examples of safety-oriented PSPMs. Plant managers and superintendents are measured against 'field time' indicators: how much time they spent out in the field (in the plant) during the week. They measure the number of field verifications done to ensure that critical controls are in place against credible fatality tasks. Checks against incident investigations are also measured, including the quality of those investigations. As Craig Wise, Superintendent Safety and Plant Protection, says, "*It really is about setting the expectation and holding your leaders to account.*" QAL has found ways to score these leading indicators so that there is a level of competitiveness between departments, which adds a bit of spice to their use.

Characteristics of an effective PSPM strategy is that the data collected is broad enough to cover the physical, social, and psychological dimensions of the safety experience, that diverse data collection methods are used, that the internal and external context surrounding the data is taken into account, and that all of this information is considered together, in order to understand the full story that the data tells.

The following PSPM self-reflection tool can be used as a guide to creating a metrics strategy appropriate for your organisation.

Positive Safety Performance Metrics

Broad data scope: The PSPMs you track should be broad enough to tap into all three dimensions of the physical, social and psychological experience of work.
Reflect on which metrics you already track within your organisation, and which further metrics are needed to provide a more thorough assessment of safety in your organisation.

Metrics examples:

Safety Culture (qualitative)		Inclusion & diversity measures	
Safety Climate (quantitative)		Work stress claims	
Safety leadership capability		Safety observations	
Safety attitudes		Critical control verifications	
Critical risk climate		Safety audits	
Wellbeing climate		% of safety issues corrected as a result of audits	
Incidents and near miss reporting		% of employees receiving OHS training	
Psychological safety climate		Error management climate	
High potential incidents		Worker engagement	
Other metrics			✓

Diverse data collection methods: Data intelligence should inform business decisions, and as such it should be based on a multitude of both qualitative and quantitative data insights not limited to safety data alone. Consider whether you have a mix of:

- Leading as well as lag indicator data
- Qualitative as well as quantitative data
- Safety-specific and non-safety-specific (HR and other) data

Consideration of context and other factors: What internal and external context factors could be influencing the attitudes and behaviours of the workforce?

Q: How might the internal organisational context be influencing safety right now? E.g., change of leadership, restructures, change projects etc)

_____

_____

Q: What external context factors may be affecting the workforce right now? E.g., the economic or political context, cultural context, regional context, etc.

_____

_____

Understanding the story: Putting the data together and viewing it through the lens of the internal and external context, what story does it tell?

_____

_____

In Chapter 6 we introduced the eight principles of positive safety and demonstrated how some of our clients are utilising each of these within their work context. Below we have included a checklist of reflection questions based on those principles that are targeted at the board and CEO. We recommend discussing these questions with your peers to support the creation of a positive safety strategy for your organisation.

Eight principles of positive safety

Board & CEO reflection questions

Principle	Reflective questions
1 Lead with a vision	Does our organisation have a clear mission and vision? What is the influence of our vision? Is it steering our organisation in the right direction? How can we use our vision to make the right decisions? Do we use our vision to guide how we reward, recognise, promote, hire, and fire? Are we positioning safety as a lever for positive culture change and transformation? Are our attitudes and behaviours as a board/CEO congruent with our vision and safety philosophy? How can we ensure the attitudes and behaviours of our senior leaders are congruent with our vision and safety philosophy?
2 Build a strong foundation	Do we have the safety systems, equipment, and resourcing required to enable our workforce to work safely and have a positive physical, social, and psychological experience of the workplace? Do we consult with the senior leadership team about what's working and what's not, and empower them to take initiatives to create a positive safety environment? How can we lead the business and make decisions that enable all safety standards to be met and go beyond meeting compliance (e.g. resourcing of people and equipment, training of leaders)?
3 Actively care	How can we demonstrate our passion and commitment for making our organisation a great place to work? How can we as an organisation demonstrate care for our workforce and build better relationships with our people? How can we empower our senior leadership team to make changes necessary so job demands are lessened? Is the board in tune with the perspective of workers in the organisation? Do we include culture in our organisational strategy?

4 Make data-based decisions	Does the data we track match our strategic objectives? What is the behavioural impact of the data we track and communicate to the organisation? Does it support a culture of learning and improvement? At a board level, do we look at assessments beyond TRIFR and LTI data (e.g. engagement surveys, turnover, exit interview summaries, safety climate, etc.) so we find the deeper story the data is telling?
5 Be curious	How can we create a culture of learning and improvement across the organisation? What avenues can we use to listen to the workforce and ask questions to ensure we are aware of issues, challenges, culture, and achievements? Where are there examples of organisational improvement in safety management within and outside of our industry? Where are there opportunities to do things differently or be bold in the way we redesign safety? How can we empower the leadership team to trial improvement strategies and innovation ideas?
6 Keep it simple	How can we ensure that the safety policy, procedures, and systems are necessary and intentional rather than a bureaucratic activity? Are we aware of the most critical physical and psychosocial risks that impact the organisation? Is our safety landscape helping or hindering safe work in the field?
7 Hunt the good stuff	How can we ensure we are aware of the great work that is being done within the organisation in regard to safety, culture and employee health, safety, and wellbeing? How can we consciously look for and recognise those people making improvements in the physical, social, and psychological experience of work?
8 Make an impact	How can we ensure we make a positive impact on our people, customers, community, and environment? How can we support our leaders to make our organisation a great place to work with a high-trust culture? Where are our opportunities to demonstrate a strong sense of corporate social responsibility?

Jobs to be done by senior leaders

Focus point 1: Demonstrated commitment to safety

Paul O'Neill would not have achieved his safety improvements at Alcoa without the support and commitment of his senior leaders at site level. Initially, it took him convincing them to achieve this – the leaders were used to being measured by throughput and quality, with safety a distant third or worse. Then, six months into his tenure, there came a terrible accident and death which O'Neill became aware of after a phone call from a plant manager in the middle of the night.

Within hours, O'Neill called all the plant's managers to the Pittsburgh head office where they joined other senior executives and spent a full day recreating what had happened and identifying all contributions to the accident. These ranged from managers who had turned a blind eye when they saw the soon-to-be victim jump over a barrier to try and unjam a machine, a lack of interlocked sensors and the likely fear in the young man that he would be blamed for the machine stopping. Finally, to make his point, O'Neill said bluntly, "*We killed this man.*" He said the death was a result of a failure of leadership on his part and of everyone else in the chain of command. Many of the leaders had assumed O'Neill's initial zeal for safety would fade away after a few weeks, as so many CEO initiatives do. Now, finally, they realised he was serious. Plant management's commitment to safety thereafter started to reflect that of O'Neill's.

Commitment to safety from senior managers is about a lot more than words. It is about perceptions, responses and, perhaps most of all, visibility. It's also about the quality of all of these. If a workforce perceives that a manager is only interested in doing audits or finding fault, they are much more likely to behave like Darren attempting to hide his cut finger injury in our earlier case study. They'll be 'safe' when someone is looking, but otherwise cut corners and fail to report incidents.

"The senior leaders at Lawson Grains regularly reflect on how they are walking the talk when it comes to their safety vision. Safety and wellbeing are always on the agenda at their farm manager sessions and annual conferences. More than that, they encourage employees to speak up about issues that are impacting them, such as fatigue management and working hours. These issues are discussed in an open forum, and leaders demonstrate their commitment to the vision by giving their people the support and resources they need, such as getting an extra headcount in peak times, so they can get the work done safely." – Robyn Heap, Lawson Grains

In our 2020 culture study,[35] there were clear shortfalls in management's commitment to safety in 51% of the surveyed sites that displayed negative safety cultures. Three clear themes emerged:

- inconsistent commitment from management
- poor prioritisation of safety
- a lack of safety leadership skills, especially role-modelling, being inspiring, motivating, and actively caring.

Often cited by workers was a belief that management staff talk the talk but don't walk the walk – especially in periods of high pressure or where production output might be compromised. Managers *say* the right things about safety, but they contradict themselves via their actions. For example, the manager who emphasises to his team that safety is the number one priority, but then questions the purchase of specialised gloves for the team, puts pressure on his frontline leaders to rush a job, or doesn't approve the extra spend to bring on additional resources to handle a particularly busy period.

Another concern raised by many frontline staff was a lack of leader visibility on site. Managers who don't make time to interact with workers in the field, both formally and informally, are sending a very clear message to workers that they are not important.

---

35 Access the Driving a Positive Safety Culture 2020 report from the List of Resources at the end of the book.

A company in regional Australia learnt this lesson the hard way. A new safety manager soon discovered concerns with safety on the frontline. A diagnostic review identified immediate risks to safety, exacerbated by a generally negative safety culture. Despite senior management having stated that safety was a core organisational value and having approved the cost of the diagnostic, they *"didn't have time"* in their busy schedules to actually hear the results.

It was a textbook example of talking the talk but failing to walk the walk. Tragically for this site, they experienced a serious incident a few months after the diagnostic, which involved one fatality and injuries to several other workers, with lasting impact on those individuals and their families along with their community and serious consequences for the company.

At those sites in our study displaying more positive safety cultures, workers felt that in addition to talking the talk, management displayed a genuine commitment to safety. They repeatedly demonstrated this by prioritising safety above production, survey respondents pointing as examples to stops in production to ensure safety, despite the financial ramification. Leaders also provided easy access to finance to purchase necessary equipment and implement strategies to ensure safe work. Senior leadership's genuine commitment was underpinned by trust and credibility, reinforced by a visible presence with frequent in-person visits into the field.

At Queensland Alumina, the idea of visibility and routine interaction is taken very seriously. The expectation is set in the plant – by the operations manager and general manager – that all superintendents and line managers will be out of their offices and in the plant between 10 and 12… *every day.* This time is blocked out in everyone's calendars. No meetings. No phone calls. No time spent answering emails.

This is time for management to be seeing for themselves what is going on in the field, checking in with and talking to operators, working with operators to identify and solve problems, carrying out investigations and ensuring that the quality of those investigations is high.

The rigorous regularity of this routine avoids walls building up between office-based management and the workers in the plant, keeping communication open, natural, and just plain normal. It builds and maintains trust between workers and leadership. Workers feel valued, they feel they have a voice, and they know that any concerns they have will be taken seriously. And if they aren't, they know there will be another opportunity to raise them the very next day – not in a week or even a month's time when their manager finally finds time to come out of their office again.

The importance of meaningful relationships with team members should not be underestimated. Positive safety cultures are created when leaders are trusted and respected by their teams. In these cultures, safety leaders establish the ground rules while granting their teams the autonomy to discover the best processes to achieve safe and productive outcomes. This was also supported by workers' perceptions that leaders genuinely want them to learn the skills needed to be able to support safety, and that they were willing to invest in this.

In contrast, poor management safety commitment erodes trust. Workers begin to feel that they are a commodity rather than a valued part of the organisation. If workers raise concerns or safety issues and hear nothing further from leadership, their only possible conclusion is that leadership doesn't care enough about them to resolve the issue. While this may not be the case, if leadership doesn't provide regular feedback to workers about issues that have been reported, the workers are left with no option but to assume nothing is happening.

Once workers start to assume that leadership doesn't value them or their safety, and there is little trust between parties, this continues to drive a negative safety culture where employees do the bare minimum required to keep their jobs. They stop raising concerns with leaders and essentially cut off communication between leadership and the frontline.

Focus point 2: Establish effective practices that support positive safety

Safety procedures are an important foundational component of safety culture, not only to meet legal obligations, but also to provide guidance on how to safely manage risks and hazards in the workplace. However, simply having procedures documented doesn't mean that they are user-friendly or effective. They need to be of good quality and actually be implemented.

This was the most common shortfall in the organisations in our 2020 study with negative safety cultures, occurring in 56% of cases. Specifically, procedures were seen to lack value or importance, or were perceived to be too complicated or difficult to implement. Procedures were often perceived as existing more to serve the company's interests than the safety of workers, their purpose being primarily to meet statutory obligations. This created a tick-and-flick mentality to following the procedures, with a ripple effect on workers' engagement with the procedures themselves and their approach to safety more broadly.

When procedures are perceived as protecting the company from possible legal action, rather than protecting people from actual risk or harm, workers are more likely to cut corners if they think they can get away with doing so. In fact, many of the workers in our study expressed the sentiment that procedures "*get in the way*" of doing their jobs.

This is true not only for frontline workers, but also for leaders who perceive the time spent completing procedure-related paperwork to be cutting into their time supervising in the field. As a result, compliance decreases. Put simply, if safety procedures aren't easy to access, easy to read and relevant for the context the employee is working within, there is a very high likelihood that they will not be followed.

This was evident in our study where workers noted that people don't always follow safety procedures because they feel swamped with too much infor-mation, they lack training in how to use the tools and processes, or because they simply don't understand the complicated 'engineer language' used in the procedures.

This last point in particular – a result of a lack of worker consultation – further perpetuates the 'us versus them' mentality so typical of negative or low maturity safety cultures. We've seen this time and again in organisations we've worked with, where procedures were written in head office by engineers who hadn't spent any meaningful time in the field. The procedures are written in complex language – sometimes referred to as 'weasel words' – that are difficult to understand, long and unnecessarily complicated. At times they are completely impractical for the employees to follow in the workplace.

An over-abundance of procedures is also common, and paradoxically it is usually a result of a 'barrier' approach to safety. When an incident occurs, the response is to put in place a new physical barrier to 'plug the hole'. Failing that, a new procedure is instituted with the same intent. When another incident occurs, the cycle repeats: another procedure to plug another hole. Over time, without careful management and review, organisations can end up with hundreds if not thousands of procedures that workers are expected to know about, understand, and follow.

A reliance on procedures isn't inherently bad for safety – recall that practices are one of the four components of our Safety Culture Model. However, it can sometimes be misguided. For example, a New Zealand client had a corporate office with a large car park. To get to the main entrance, workers needed to walk to the far right of the car park and then follow a long and cumbersome pedestrian pathway. This also meant crossing the entire car park and, during peak periods, navigating incoming and outgoing vehicles.

As humans, our brains love to save energy, so we often look for the shortest way to achieve our goals. In this case, the shortest path was to walk through a small garden bed that divided the car park from the building. Most employees took this route every day, so much so that the garden bed had eroded into a makeshift path. The company was aware of the shortcut and likely saw the risk as low or non-existent, so turned a blind eye to the behaviour.

One day, an employee tripped while walking through the garden bed, falling, and breaking her nose. She had to have both corrective and cosmetic surgery as a result. The company's response wasn't to create a safer, more practical route for their people; instead they built a fence around the garden.

Sometimes in their haste to prevent an incident from reoccurring, organisations fail to see how impractical or unhelpful the proposed solution might be – especially when they haven't considered all the data or consulted the workers who carry out the task on the frontline.

While responsibility for the establishment of procedures will typically fall to the safety manager and their team, ensuring that those procedures are relevant, understood and used is the joint responsibility of all senior management. It is the leadership's visible and active support of the procedures and the reasons for them that will raise them to the level of importance required for them to play a lasting role in safety management.

There is another point that needs to be made about procedures from the perspective of three-dimensional safety. Recall that three-dimensional safety encompasses the physical, social, and psychological experiences of people at work.

Many existing safety procedures were developed in one-dimensional safety cultures, with a focus almost entirely on preventing physical harm. Some may have had references to psychological harm included to bring them up to date.

Procedures in a safe, three-dimensional safety environment need to go a few steps further than that if they are to truly provide a safe, well and engaged workforce. They also need to move away from the tick-and-flick style of procedure, becoming *practices* that are more subjective and focused on education and awareness.

For instance, at Queensland Alumina, they encourage their leaders to consider 'activator, behaviour and consequence' in their interactions with people (a model similar to our ABR model – attitude, behaviour, results). Craig Wise shared an example of a six-foot-five (196 centimetre) supervisor approaching a coaching conversation with a new, slightly built, female employee.

Aware that his physical size, regardless of anything else, could be intimidating for the young woman, the supervisor actively rounded his shoulders to make himself smaller. In the conversation, he directed his eyes more at the equipment they were talking about rather than looking down on the woman.

All of this led to a stronger engagement between the two and ultimately a more impactful conversation. This is a good example of a practice that would be hard to capture in a black-and-white procedure, and a practice that was only specifically relevant in the particular circumstance of this large man talking to a much smaller worker.

"The best way to record this sort of thing is not to record it at all," says Craig. It's more about setting an expectation and trusting people to meet that expectation. It is one of the truest examples of positive safety in which the culture surpasses the need for wholesale reliance on documented procedures.

Focus point 3: Change management

Rod Maule, General Manager of Safety and Wellbeing at Australia Post, has an impressive background in senior safety leadership roles and change management in large organisations, building on an early career as a strategic marketing manager and national franchise manager for BP. Rod shared with us his unique expertise using stakeholder management and cross-functional collaboration to aid change management success.

Rod sees the inclusion of stakeholders at the earliest opportunity as critical to the success of any change initiative, safety or otherwise.

"We are often developing safety initiatives that involve an external consultant or a company like Sentis. However, if the stakeholders aren't buying in, the initiative will fail. It's not about how smart the person is or how well intentioned the program is. The critical factor is the ability to get buy in and therefore successful execution from the people that the initiative impacts. You might be better off to go with Plan B if it's got better buy-in, rather than go with Plan A that has no buy-in."

It seems obvious, but being clear about the 'why' of the change at the outset is really important.

"Part of change management is working through what the problem is that you're trying to fix, and being really clear on that, then working through what is going on with the context and how the context impacts your stakeholders. As a senior person in an organisation, what I want to try to give my people is context and priorities. I want the same from my own bosses. Context and priorities inform the approach we need to take, the budget we need and which stakeholders we need engaged. When we have a clear context and priorities, we can deliver on the execution."

Governance is also critical in providing stakeholder management and keeping the critical players working collaboratively and closely on the project over time.

"As an example, one of the big projects we've been working on at Australia Post recently involved a partnership with Google using machine learning. Essentially, it is about training our digital cameras at our major facilities to recognise the difference between people and our mobile plant components, and teaching it to recognise hazards, boundaries, and the difference between safe and unsafe work zones. We've had fabulous success with that project.

"What helped in getting that project through in the organisation is that we had all the GMs accountable. The head of security was involved because the project is connected to all the security cameras. The head of IT was necessary because we needed a lot of IT support to get the project up and running. The general managers of operations for the various businesses and me as the general manager of safety also had to be closely involved. So together we made up the governance group.

"This governance group was able to smash through a lot of the bureaucracy that would otherwise have had us bogged down for months. Because we were the stakeholders, we could say, 'Hey, I'm stuck here,' or, 'No problem, I can make that a priority; I'll make that go away.' So we got that project through really successfully. We met weekly, and we overcame a lot of the barriers that a lower-level group would have gotten stuck with.

"This project has resulted in a 95 to 98% reduction in exposure of people breaching those processes. And it's been sustained for two to three years… We've since iterated on that pilot, and we've now rolled it out to 30 major facilities. We're also using the thinking behind that project in another project we've been doing as well."

Another factor here is collaboration, particularly in an area like safety that traditionally sits on the side of operations in a support role. Coming in from 'outside' and throwing out current programs or initiatives is always a high-risk strategy because it can disengage stakeholders very quickly. Rod concurs,

"You need to bring people along on the journey. I always look for the things we are doing elsewhere in the organisation, and look at how we build safety into them, rather than have safety separate. The way I work is to collaborate and bring those other stakeholders in, rather than compete. The more you can collaborate, the better."

There are many layers to successful change management – we could write a whole book on this topic alone, as many have already done – but the points Rod makes provide initial fundamentals that can't be overlooked. Without stakeholder engagement and cross-functional collaboration throughout, any significant change is likely to fall short of expectations.

Eight principles of positive safety

Senior leader reflection questions

Principle	Reflective questions
1 Lead with a vision	How does our vision resonate with our workforce? Is it inspiring and positively received? How can we link behaviours, performance, reward, and recognition to our vision? How can we ensure the attitudes and behaviours of our frontline leaders are congruent with our vision and safety philosophy?
2 Build a strong foundation	Do our frontline leaders have the skills, capability, and capacity to engage with the systems that have been provided and lead a positive safety approach? Do we understand the user experience of our safety systems? How can we ensure safety training and safety initiatives are embedded and supported to increase training effectiveness? Do our people understand the critical risks and know how to manage them? How effectively does collaboration occur across teams?
3 Actively care	How do we demonstrate active care to our leaders and workers (including contractors) within the organisation? Do we demonstrate care by upholding safety as a core value? How do the decisions we make and the priorities we set communicate our care and influence our people? Are we growing people with the right values into new roles and responsibilities? How can we connect with our people, build strong relationships, and understand their needs and wants?
4 Make data-based decisions	Are we tracking helpful data and focusing on 'good' data rather than unreliable or invalid data? How can we reduce the focus on TRIFR, LTIs and the tick & flick culture? How can we use data to understand, act, make changes, and do things differently? Do we augment the safety data with other essential metrics e.g. near misses, safety audits and inspections, critical control verifications, infield safety coaching, safety climate, wellbeing, etc? What data do we need to focus on, in order to create a culture of learning and improvement?

5 Be curious	How confident are we that we are hearing about potential issues and problems within the organisation? What systems and/or processes do we need to put in place so we are able to encourage reporting, capture the learnings, and communicate it across the business? How effective are our processes to gather and manage employee feedback and suggestions? How often do we actively seek feedback? What processes do we use to ensure the feedback loop is closed?
6 Keep it simple	How do workers experience the safety procedures and systems? Are the procedures and administrative side of safety getting in the way of safe attitudes and behaviours? If so, what could be done? How can we encourage leaders to take initiative and solve safety challenges, simplify systems and procedures, and keep messages simple and aligned with the vision and safety goals?
7 Hunt the good stuff	Are we seeing our people as an army of problem solvers, or an army of problems? What reward and recognition initiatives have we put in place to encourage positive safety behaviours? Do we focus on the absence of safety and things going wrong, or do we consciously look for the presence of safety and notice all the great work our leaders and teams are doing? How can we acknowledge and recognise the great work of leaders and their teams and celebrate the wins?
8 Make an impact	How can we provide opportunities for our workforce to make a positive impact on our people, customers, community, and environment? How can we invest in improving the organisational culture so that work has a positive impact on the wellbeing of our employees? E.g. through leadership capability uplift, giving leaders the time and capacity to be visible, building relationships and hearing the challenges and solutions of people across the business, and being bold enough to change the design of work where necessary? How does our organisation support employees to build connections across different departments and teams?

Jobs to be done by frontline leaders

Before we discuss the actions of frontline leaders in promoting a positive safety culture, we need to emphasise that the actions we've just described at board/CEO level and executive level are *prerequisites* for what follows. Don't expect change to come or be driven by frontline leaders without the absolute and active support of the layers of leadership above them. Paul O'Neill understood this very well: it was why he called in all his executive managers after a fatal accident and shared responsibility for the incident with them. No one was allowed to pass the buck down to frontline managers.

Focus point 1: Building trust

While senior leaders play a critical role in creating and sponsoring a vision for positive safety, frontline leaders play a role of equal importance in the creation and maintenance of the necessary habits that underpin a positive safety culture. This makes trust between these leaders and their teams paramount. Our research showed that positive safety cultures are created when leaders are genuinely trusted and respected by their teams.

While many books have been written about trust in leadership, at its core it is pretty simple. When a leader sees themselves as a team member, while also accepting responsibility for the team as a whole, their crew is much more likely to follow them. This means being accessible, including spending significant time on the floor or in the field. It means working alongside their team members, cooperatively solving problems together. It means acting as a channel for communications up and down the chain, advocating for the team to senior management and explaining (as best they can) decision-making from up the line.

All of this applies to safety culture as much as it does the broader team culture. Frontline leaders need to keep safety front of mind on a day-to-day basis, in between any efforts coming from more senior management. They need to amplify the senior management vision, dedicating frequent and regular time to specific safety walks and critical control verifications. Perhaps above all else, they need to ensure that communication lines around safety remain clear and open in all directions, including between team members.

"I've learnt that in just spending time with people, listening to them, and having conversations over time, we can establish strong relation-ships, which re-engaged them in safety and has them wanting to make a difference. This approach has completely turned stores around from a safety and wellbeing perspective." – Bennjamin Mathews, Kmart

Our study found that effective communication was a strength for 50% of sites operating with a positive or close-to-positive safety culture. At these sites, workers held positive perceptions of safety briefings such as pre-starts, toolbox talks, meetings, and workshops. They talked about safety briefings occurring frequently, high attendance rates, engaging communication, and both permanent and contract workers contributing to discussions.

The most positive sites found safety briefings to be both useful and relevant, with a strong emphasis on ensuring workers were adequately briefed prior to starting jobs. Critical to this – and a key difference in comparison to more negative cultures – was the encouragement of two-way communi-cation and worker participation. Rather than a lecture or brisk tick-and-flick activity, supervisors actively encouraged open discussion about safety hazards and controls, as well as emphasising improvements and lessons learnt.

To further encourage active participation, leaders used strategies such as asking helpful questions, empowering the team members to lead and drive the discussions themselves, sharing relevant videos, using activities, or using current events at the site or in the news to make safety discussions relevant and interesting.

"[In the past], there was a safety officer who would go around, do investigations, do inspections and audits, and provide a long list of

everything that was wrong with a store. We changed that role to be focused on getting in there and building relationships with the leaders in stores. It was about getting to know them, what motivated them, what made them tick, what were the challenges, what were their strengths in their store, while also keeping a part of our role as finding hazards and keeping people safe." – Bennjamin Mathews

Some workers also mentioned informal communication as an important contributor to workplace safety. This type of communication is where teams choose to talk about safety even when it isn't formalised or required of them. The use of radios to keep in touch and update progress throughout the shift also allowed teams to keep safety messages front of mind beyond the pre-start meeting. The more often our brains hear information, the more likely that information will stick.

Consider the supervisor who asks his team to look out for an upcoming change to the traffic management plan during pre-start one morning. Instead of leaving it there, he asks his team to communicate with one another throughout the day to keep everyone in the loop regarding any changes. As the day goes on, different workers share information regarding the development. Due to these small but regular reminders, every worker keeps the upcoming change front of mind.

It is unsurprising that the psychological safety experience is particularly affected by the trust people have in their frontline leaders. *"The most important influence on psychological safety is the nearest boss,"* says Professor Amy Edmondson, an expert on psychological safety. As humans, our brains crave social environments in which we feel safe, trusting those around us and particularly those who lead us. When this condition is met, our motivation to contribute to our group in a positive way soars. We see people demonstrating care, taking ownership, and giving their best at work – all ideal safety citizenship behaviours.

All this tends to work best, and to reinforce a positive safety culture, when the frontline leader's style is empowering and participative; the leader establishing the ground rules then trusting their team with enough autonomy to discover the best processes to achieve safe and productive outcomes. This requires sustained effort from the leader.

Think of trust as a tide that ebbs and flows with the interactions you have in the workplace. Even if you've got strong levels of trust in your workplace, you need to actively ensure that you're maintaining this trust by keeping open lines of communication and holding yourself to the same standards of behaviour. A little conscious action is all it takes to prevent the tide of trust from receding.

Focus point 2: Creating a learning culture around incident reporting

Effective reporting of incidents – from near misses to minor injuries to psychological threats and worse – is fundamental to a positive safety culture. Aside from the human element (if someone gets hurt, they need to be cared for), incident reports provide critical insight into real-life risks and genuine opportunities for improvement. Reporting incidents creates invaluable learning opportunities, allowing organisations to adapt, make improvements, and prevent future injury. If leaders don't understand the types of incidents occurring in their businesses, they can't put measures in place to prevent them.

All too often, however, incidents go unreported. In 2018, Sentis carried out a study into the culture of underreporting. Our research indicated that, conservatively, 25% of incidents were going unreported globally, with the figure at over 30% in Australia. Specifically, we found that approximately half of the workers surveyed experienced at least one incident in the prior 12 months. Of these, 30% failed to report an average of 6.3 incidents over a 12 month period. In practice, this can mean that an organisation of 3,000 employees sees over 2,800 unreported incidents in a year – a staggering number of missed opportunities to make things safer. The predominant reasons for failing to report were under-appreciation of the importance of reporting and fear that reporting would have negative consequences for the messenger.

As we have explained, humans are naturally socially conscious beings, which makes the reporting of incidents a fraught issue for management. While we're not advocating that workers should be calling the CEO at home to report a serious incident, as Paul O'Neill encouraged at Alcoa, what is true is that managers – at all levels – need to create an atmosphere of awareness and openness that encourages incident reporting and in which people feel safe doing so. Worker willingness to report incidents and errors in an accurate and timely manner is a vitally important characteristic of a positive safety culture.

As we saw earlier in this book with the case of Darren and his cut finger, workers are often afraid of being blamed by others for an incident. They might feel discomfort at the idea of a permanent blemish on their record, or of peer disapproval for the loss of a safety bonus. In short, unless the working environment leaves employees feeling safe, well, and engaged, there's a good chance that many incidents will go unreported.

Instead of motivating a team to report potential safety issues, an approach to investigation that doesn't address this discomfort – this psychosocial risk – leads to a mindset of, 'If I can hide it, I will'. No matter what pressure they are feeling from above, the frontline leader needs to remember that the real enemy is the source of the risk, not the employee reporting it. Using positive reinforcement to associate a sense of accomplishment and reward with the act of safety reporting will shift the motivation within your team from the controlled 'I report because I have to' to the autonomous 'I report because I want to'.

This does require constant reassurance from frontline and other managers, consistently demonstrating that reporting an incident doesn't have negative consequences for the person doing the reporting, nor for anyone else. They must ensure that reporting is made easy and that reported incidents are actively taken seriously, properly escalated, and followed up – that workers see a tangible outcome as a result of being courageous enough to make a report. This encourages more reporting in future.

In contrast, cumbersome reporting systems and processes and a lack of action or feedback from leadership following a report were common sources of discouragement revealed in our research, and these perpetuate cultures of underreporting.

This is a particular concern for very large corporate businesses. The earlier example from Bennjamin Mathews at Kmart, in which team members did not have access to the incident reporting system and so could not formally report an incident without relying on their supervisor, is not atypical. Obviously, with a sound relationship between worker and supervisor, this indirect reporting would not present a problem and in fact it could help create a learning opportunity out of the situation. However, where the worker/supervisor relationship is not strong, and particularly where the worker might fear being blamed for the incident, this need for indirect reporting can become a barrier and lead to underreporting.

The best case scenario here is that not only are all incidents transparently and honestly reported, but that they become genuine learning opportunities, not opportunities to attribute blame. Here again, though, the investigation following a report needs to be conducted in a manner that is genuinely interested in identifying the reasons for the incident.

Considering all factors of the Safety Culture Model (people, practices, environment, and leadership) in your incident investigations is a good start. If the investigation keeps pointing to people as the root cause, review your incident investigation process. It is rarely just one person's decision, independent of external factors, that is the primary contributor to an incident.

A significant component of success in this area is the training of frontline leaders in safety management and, within that, worker engagement, leading to an improved safety experience and so on, building up to the ideal level of safety citizenship.

Focus point 3: Building on positive behaviour

Safety responsibility

We use the term 'safety responsibility' to refer to the discretionary effort workers display in relation to safety activities, their acceptance and ownership of their safety duties, and the relationship they have with the health and safety team and other workgroups. A strong level of safety responsibility is one of the defining factors of a positive safety culture.

Safety responsibility was a strength in at least half the sites in our study that displayed positive or near-positive safety cultures. Characteristics of these sites included that:

- employees took safety practices seriously
- employees were open to feedback regarding safety
- safety was considered a core part of each person's job
- employees understood the importance of safety and accepted safety as their own personal responsibility
- employees felt empowered to stop unsafe work
- the health and safety teams were seen to support safe work.

These workers saw safety responsibilities as a core part of every person's role and took personal responsibility for their own safety and that of others. Teams and crews at all levels showed belief in the importance of sustained vigilance to both detect and control hazards. Additionally, they were open to feedback regarding their safety.

When coached on how to make safer choices, they received feedback positively, genuinely appreciating the concern for their safety. In these environments, taking safety practices seriously – such as wearing PPE, following procedures, and stopping unsafe work – was a natural way of operating. They didn't need to be supervised or instructed.

In positive safety cultures, safety responsibility isn't discussed – it just 'is'. There is an internal and personal motivation to make a choice for safety and to speak up for safety. Workers feel empowered to not only identify and address hazards in their own work and that of others, but to also 'stop the line' when a safety issue becomes apparent and threatens potential harm. Importantly, the health and safety team is seen as a source of support rather than a source of fear (i.e. the safety police), as is more commonly the case on sites with negative cultures.

Team support is central here. It relates to the quality of relationships between team members, the level of care and concern for each other, and the willingness to confront a co-worker who violates safety standards. It includes behaviours like looking out for each other, encouraging each other and being willing to help out. Safety is seen as a team effort through which people work together to keep each other safe.

Confronting a co-worker if they are seen engaging in a potentially risky or unsafe behaviour is regarded as par for the course. In fact 'confronting' is probably too strong a word; it's really just a matter of pointing out the risk and sharing ideas to ameliorate it, with the first person being thankful that their colleague raised the issue. Similarly, there is no hesitation in stopping work immediately if something or someone is not acting safely, and not resuming until it is safe to do so.

Whilst raising the alarm in these ways needs to be part of the wider organisational culture around safety, there is no doubt that frontline managers play an important role in supporting and maintaining them in the field. The frontline manager will normally be the first line of decision making, especially when the pressure is on and a decision around safety might compromise a critical production target.

It is worth noting that at more positive sites, high team support for safety often leads to informal buddy or mentoring systems for new employees and a tendency for workers to assist each other to complete tasks in a safe way. This concern and support can extend beyond formal tasks, with workers looking out for each other when they feel they might be struggling either mentally or physically. These practices can also be encouraged and supported by frontline leaders.

The strongest predictor of team safety responsibility is a frontline leader who effectively role models safety and actively demonstrates how much they value the importance of positive safety behaviours. Being a role model for the safe attitudes and behaviours you want to see in your team builds trust, shows commitment, and increases reciprocal behaviours from others. Some of the things frontline leaders can do include:

- Beyond formal safety briefings, actively engage workers in informal settings (e.g. lunch breaks) to discuss their workplace safety experiences.
- Set a positive safety example at all times by being attentive at safety inductions, adhering to all safety procedures and always ensuring that you're wearing the appropriate PPE yourself. Nothing undermines safety protocols more than senior people who ignore them. Failing to wear ear or eye protection for even a short visit onto the factory floor is a surefire way to signal that you regard these precautions as trivial.
- Actively contribute to and be involved in any safety training and reviews to reinforce the understanding that you value operational safety.
- Report any safety hazards or incidents as soon as they arise, regardless of the inconveniences that the process might have.

In short, live and breathe safety yourself. Then make sure you notice when others do the same and praise that behaviour.

Hunting the good stuff

Why would a person turn up to work with a broken leg? Or deliberately risk their own safety in order to increase production output? It's often about measurement and reward.

The way workers are recognised for their performance around safety can have a substantial effect on their perception of the authenticity with which an organisation addresses and prioritises safety and on their consequent behaviours.

At one refinery we worked with, workers were rewarded for production success with monetary bonuses, but when they achieved a year free of lost-time injuries, they received a chocolate bar at the gate on their way home. In this case, the message to the workforce was clear: we value production far more highly than we value safety.

This was reflected in our study. On sites with negative safety cultures, it was common to hear that reward and recognition strategies were directly tied to production, not safety. It may not be the intention – it probably isn't – but an arrangement like this naturally encourages a culture of production over safety, rather than one of safe production. In fact, it can have the opposite effect and drive counterproductive safety behaviours by, perhaps inadvertently, rewarding the cutting of corners or choice of unsafe practices.

Even when incentives are aimed at safety specifically, the wrong incentives can have unintended consequences. On a number of sites in our study, the achievement of safety performance measures was linked to monetary incentives. It's not difficult to predict worker behaviour when a bonus is on the line. We have heard many stories of people failing to report incidents in order to preserve a financial bonus. Hence the mention of the broken leg: in one extreme case, a person literally turned up to work with a broken leg, sitting in the office all day so that his injury wasn't classed as an LTI.

Of course, flawed as they are, even these examples are better than the still common use of a 'stick' approach to safety. A fear-based and punitive approach, in which team members are punished for breaking safety protocols, not only hinders safety performance but it affects performance generally. The problem is that while punishment can lead to a change in behaviour, it doesn't always change the behaviour that you want to change.

As the earlier case of Darren illustrated, punishing a worker for not complying with safety procedures may drive them to not report future incidents so they don't get caught again, rather than change their level of compliance.

The implication here for the frontline manager is the need to hunt for the good stuff: to look out for and reward positive behaviours. Importantly, the provision of positive feedback needs to significantly outweigh any negative feedback team members might be receiving from either the manager themselves or any other part of the business.

As humans, we have a natural tendency to weigh negative information more heavily than positive information – something psychologists call 'negativity bias'.[36] In simple terms, this means that our brains remember and are more heavily influenced by negative events and experiences than positive ones. Perhaps you remember receiving a negative comment (or what you perceived as a negative comment) from a teacher about a piece of work you did at school. Do you remember mulling over that comment far more than any number of positive comments you received from that same teacher? If you have children, you might have seen them having a similar experience. We do the same on the road. That driver who cut you off leaves you steaming for much longer than the nice feeling of numerous other drivers courteously allowing you to merge. If you've ever run workshops with feedback sheets, you likely took the single negative response to heart far more than all the positive responses put together.

Negativity bias is hardwired into our brains. It's another one of those safety mechanisms, like 'fight or flight'. Forgetting about a negative or potentially harmful circumstance increases the likelihood of us being in that situation again, increasing the chances of us getting injured or worse. This applies to both physical and social situations. It's why we only have to put our hand on a hot stove once in our lives, and why (most of us) learn the art of being tactful in our social relationships from a fairly early age. Positive experiences, on the other hand, make us feel warm and fuzzy, but warm and fuzzy is not a feeling that we need to keep ourselves safe.

It follows that in the workplace, negative interactions or situations that trigger a fear response have a more significant and lasting impact on

---

36 (Baumeister et al., 2001)

workers than positive interactions. Even if most leaders have a strong track record of maintaining positive relationships with the workforce, one major negative interaction can be enough to turn the tide.

Traditionally, safety management is a prime source of negativity. What do organisations typically spend more time focusing on when it comes to safety? When things go wrong, they look for the absence of safety, not the presence of safety. If they have a run of injury-free months, there might be some acknowledgement, but it will soon be crowded out by other issues. But when someone gets injured, or there's a near miss, or they miss a KPI, everyone hears about it. Now safety is the *primary* issue!

Most safety programs suggest that leaders should not walk past an unsafe act or situation without pointing it out. Superficially, that does seem logical: they do want to correct unsafe behaviours and prevent potential incidents. The problem is that if they *only* point out what's wrong, being safe becomes almost tiresome. The motivation to be safe is all controlled, 'I have to' motivation.

The way to turn this around is to proactively focus on the positives. Start noticing and commenting on everything your team is doing right when it comes to safety. Not just the numbers, but the behaviours. Not even just compliance, but positive safety behaviours like looking out for each other, making good choices, and taking the initiative on safety.

The more focus there is on these positives, the more people will feel good about safety and their role in it. Their motivation will be increasingly of the autonomous 'I want to' variety. In this atmosphere, if someone is noticed doing the wrong thing, or a hazard is pointed out, that feedback will be taken in good spirit instead of being yet another weight on the shoulders. When considering how to provide positive reinforcement most effectively, think *strategic*, *specific*, and *targeted*:

- Be *strategic* by being conscious of the behaviours and attitudes you want to see, rather than providing feedback in a generic way that may not be seen as authentic. Have a clear vision of the safety culture you are working towards in your particular area, and then look for and publicly acknowledge behaviours consistent with that culture.

- In line with being strategic, make sure the feedback you provide is also *specific*. In other words, share what it was that you saw as a positive, rather than simply saying *"Good job,"* or *"Thanks for that."* For example, *"Hey Bob, thanks for showing Tony how to get that job done without having to remove his safety glasses. I really appreciate your willingness to look out for others in that way."* Being specific will have a much more sustainable effect on behaviour change.

- To be effective in the long-term, *target* any recognition or rewards at the intrinsic motivations of each individual team member. To do this, you need to get to know your people and find out what is valuable to them. For some, it might be the opportunity to learn a new skill or attend a development program. For others, it may be the chance to take on tasks that will broaden their career horizons. Some will enjoy public acknowledgment while others might prefer private thanks.

Eight principles of positive safety

Frontline leader reflection questions

Principle	Reflective questions
1 Lead with a vision	How can I communicate the vision to my team and ensure it is sufficiently relevant to them that they can see their role in it? How can we link tasks/activities/projects to the vision? How can I use the vision to clarify our safety expectations and paint a clear picture of what good looks like? How can we reward attitudes and behaviours that are aligned to the vision?
2 Build a strong foundation	Do my team members have the skills, capability, and capacity to engage with the systems that have been provided? Does my team demonstrate positive safety behaviours e.g. housekeeping, risk assessments, wearing of PPE, setting up barricading, reporting incidents, fatigue management, correct application of critical controls? What is the user experience of our safety systems and procedures like for my team?
3 Actively care	How do I demonstrate active care to my team members? Am I aware of the challenges or situations that could be negatively impacting my team members' physical, social, or psychological experience of their jobs? Do I take action accordingly and close the feedback loop? Is the climate within my team conducive to positive safety? How can I bring out the best in my team by allowing them autonomy and control regarding how they conduct their tasks and make decisions?
4 Make data-based decisions	Does my team understand the safety metrics and targets and why we measure them? How can I link the safety metrics back to the intention that we all go home safe and well, and remain engaged? What might get in the way of my team accurately reporting important safety data such as hazards, near misses, and mistakes?

5 Be curious	How can I demonstrate active care, supportiveness and show that we play the ball, not the person, in order to encourage reporting? How can we make incidents opportunities to grow and learn? How do people experience reporting? Where are my opportunities to spend time in the field talking to the people doing the work, recognising them as the experts in their jobs, and finding out about the roadblocks and gaps between work as imagined and work as done?
6 Keep it simple	Does my team understand all the safety procedures and processes they interact with on the job? What is the user-experience of the procedures and processes? How can I make it better? How could the system be simplified and improved? What great ideas do my team members have on how their experience of safe work and safety reporting could be improved?
7 Hunt the good stuff	Where are there opportunities to reinforce the helpful attitudes and positive safety behaviour within my team? How can I help shift the attitude from 'The safety police are just there to catch us doing the wrong thing' to 'The safety people are there to see us doing the right thing, and support us when there's a gap between work as imagined and work as done'? How would my employees like to be recognised for safe behaviour? What rewards or recognition are successfully motivating employees in other areas? What motivates my people most effectively?
8 Make an impact	How can we give a line of sight to the positive impact we are having on our people, customers, community, and environment? How can we ensure work has a positive impact on our individual team members? How can I build a culture within my team that helps to ensure work has a positive impact on the wellbeing of my team members?

8.
UNITYWATER: SHIFTING TOWARDS THE POSITIVE SAFETY APPROACH

"Success is not final, failure is not fatal:
It is the courage to continue that counts."

~Winston Churchill

Unitywater is a utility company providing water supply and sewage treatment services to Queensland's Sunshine Coast and surrounding areas. We have worked with the business for a number of years on their journey towards positive safety and safety citizenship. Kenan Hibberd, Executive Manager – People, Culture and Safety, has been with the organisation for a decade and has overseen significant progress along that journey of this period.

"When I first joined this business 10 years ago, we were heavily focused on injury management and rehabilitation. This reflected a very immature state as an organisation. It's obvious you have a

*problem when your scorecard is being marked by how you are
returning people to work – especially how quickly and effectively you
are rehabilitating injury. But that was the primary focus of the organisation at that point…*

*"We were chasing to try and eliminate all risk and achieve zero harm.
We were working in what you would call a very physical environment
and looking at 'If something goes wrong, and people get hurt, how
do we manage that effectively?' [The focus was on] building a safety
management system to try and control and prevent risk."*

The business's safety record improved with better management, but the
pattern was the same as that we have described a number of times in this
book. They were in *"pretty poor shape"* with an LTI rate of around 29 (per
month) initially, which they were able to bring down to around 12 and then
below double digits.

*"But we would always then regress back into a spate of injuries. We
would go six to seven months in a year without any issues, and then
all of a sudden we'd have six or seven."*

This presented a challenge to Kenan and the other senior management. The
business carries a high level of risk, much of their work involving construction of infrastructure along with the chemical processing work of treatment
plants. *"We've got construction, maintenance, mechanical, electrical. We've
got all the psychological risks that go with intense project work."* In addition,
they have a large maintenance team that spends many hours on the road
moving between different facilities.

In response to the levelling off of safety performance, senior management
started to ask themselves how they could create what we would call a more
mature safety environment.

*"We started to [ask ourselves] how we could start to create an
environment where people think and act and behave in a way that's*

actually safe, because they feel like they're valued and appreciated by the organisation and they understand that we genuinely have a common interest. We started to look at the cultural elements of the business.

"We were pretty confident we could do all the mechanical stuff and manage that as well as any other organisation [because] we were a genuinely well-intended employer that really wanted to look after its people. [We wanted to] give our people a good experience and keep them safe, but we weren't necessarily giving them that good experience."

Early diagnostic work commissioned by Kenan highlighted a safety culture characterised by fear and blame. People felt that they would be blamed if something went wrong, which was setting them on edge. *"This permeated through all parts of our business and our relationships and our interactions."* People felt that the organisation valued their experience of work, but only as far as that did not compromise efficiency. Operational performance improvement and cost reduction were the priorities.

The culture data told Kenan and his team that teams within the business *"felt a strong sense of support and care for each other and their leaders,"* but they weren't feeling that way about the wider organisation.

Further culture assessment identified that they *"had a business that was used to convention – just follow the rules, don't do anything that you're not supposed to do... – that sort of stuff."* They recognised that this was probably a result of both the industry they were in and the company's history as a government utility prior to corporatisation. An Onsite Safety Evaluation assessing Unitywater's safety maturity facilitated by Sentis *"put our organisation squarely down at the level of counterproductive."*

From this information and a commitment to taking a safety maturity journey, Unitywater worked with Sentis and others to develop a program to influence behaviours they called 'Switch on to Shape' (or 'Shape'), which communicated the opportunity to collectively shape the culture they wanted in the business. In making this decision, they were putting safety at the vanguard of their foray into a wider cultural change. A safer work environment would help build a better work environment generally.

One of the blockages to improvement that was identified early on was an emphasis on compliance.

> "We previously had this view that if individuals breached safety provisions, these things called 'life saving rules', they would be subject to disciplinary action. This was one that we thought was contra to what we were trying to achieve out of Shape. So, we reset the expectations around that to say that if people made mistakes, or if people actually did the wrong thing, but what they've done is simply to follow their custom and the practice of the organisation, then there's no more disciplinary stuff. It's about learning why they're trying to do that."

Discipline was restricted to specific circumstances, such as wilful damage or malicious behaviour.

> "That was where we started to see some positive shift [culturally]. But in our injury data and our incident data, we were continually getting this decline and improvement, and then we'd still hit a point where we'd bounce back up… and that was the thing we had started this journey to try and address. [That was when] the board started to voice their concerns. They had made a significant investment in this initiative, and wanted to see the benefits coming through in our data."

Kenan and his team knew improvement was happening – they could see it on the ground – but they weren't seeing it in the crude safety numbers. Specifically, they were hampered by the reliance on TRIFR as a key performance indicator. It was at this point that Unitywater strengthened its approach to the management of high-risk activities through an in-depth review of all incidents that had serious injury or fatality potential (SIFp –

also known as high-potential near misses).[37]

> *"TRIFR is a very blunt instrument that doesn't give you any real cor-relation around the severity of injury or the risks in your business. It's useful to compare sectors, but beyond that, there's not much value. So, we did this Meta Incident Analysis®. [We took] five years of data to the team at Sentis and their partners at Incident Analytics: injury data, incident data, near misses, hazards. Every single thing we could pull out. One of the benefits of Unitywater is that we actually did have a pretty good reporting culture in spite of our sort of fear and blame type approach, so we had extensive information available to be interrogated.*

> *"The first thing we were able to do was identify what the critical risks were within the organisation. We were able to say, 'These are the high potential [risks] that Unitywater actually has; these are the 10 key things,' and we were then able to [show that the] actual rate of those high potentials had declined over that five-year journey."*

114 incidents (16.6%) were considered potential serious injury & fatality (SIFp) events and were then subject to detailed analysis.

1000+ hazards were explored for weak signals to eventual incidents.

50% of SIFp incidents involved motor vehicle usage.

---

37 Access the full case study report, 'Major Utilities Company Discovers an Opportunity for Improved Serious Incident Focus' in the List of Resources at the end of the book.

The analysis also uncovered some interesting yearly trends.

- 1.0% reduction in work hours lost year on year.
- 7.5% reduction in recordable incidents ('vehicle incident' and 'injury' event categories) year on year.
- 7.0% increase in near misses reported year on year (note 32% of SIFp incidents were categorised as 'near miss').
- 34.2% reduction in SIFp Incident Exposure year on year, demonstrating ROI on safety initiatives.

Through these numbers, Kenan could demonstrate that the organisation was in fact getting safer and that despite what the TRIFR numbers were saying, the number of significant incidents was declining also. This was confirmation that the investment in safety was paying off after all.

"Another learning out of this was [the benefit of] sharpening our focus as an organisation to really look at the things that matter – the things that are going to kill, maim, or have a life-changing event for an individual in this business, one of our contracting partners or a member of the public.

"We believed we would get more value out of focusing on those things and how frequently they occur and how well we have controlled them, rather than on every single low consequence injury that occurs. The ones [for which] we used to have a Royal Commission to basically interrogate why poor old Bob had strained a calf muscle stepping out of a truck, when he's 58 years of age! No wonder people didn't want to talk to us about stuff."

Not only were time and effort spent on these investigations unproductive, it annoyed those injured, who also saw it as a waste of time. However, rather than ignore these injuries altogether, attention was turned to targeted programs, such as a transitionary program for ageing workers and manual handling, while the main focus switched to the more significant incidents.

"My advice would be always [to tackle] the full data set at both ends. Our board drew a lot of comfort from this, and they [started to] see the place getting better. The other thing was that by focusing on high potentials and taking out all those conversations and time and effort spent on low consequence stuff, you sharpen up the focus of everyone in the business. You make everyone feel better because you're actually looking at things that really count. What we saw was people started to relax and to be more engaged in the process of incident management and review."

Meanwhile, for the less significant incidents and injuries, there was appreciation from frontline leaders that they were being trusted to deal with the system of work themselves.

The sharper focus also revealed some previously overlooked blind spots, such as the number of traffic injuries. It turned out that the team driving a collective five million kilometres a year was the most risky work function of the business. Another was the risk of animal attack: snakes, ticks, and domestic dogs.

This investigation process revealed several recommendations.

System improvements

Implement immediate improvements in critical control management for high risk activities (with priority on motor vehicles, contact with electricity, working at heights hazardous substances, confined spaces and animal attack / lone field worker).

Enable the frontline

Improve understanding of critical controls and engagements of crew in high-risk work.

Leadership capability and involvement

Strengthen capacity, capability and role clarity for operational leadership roles.

Governance

Introduce leading indicators for improving and assuring critical control management.

The major outcome of this renewed focus was a shift in the next intervention around critical controls.

> "It's our part of a wider thing called 'Creating better and safer together', which is about the culture program as well as the safety piece. It's all intermeshed with safety at the heart of our organisational capabilities. As a leader, I know my obligations, I know how we want to behave and how we want to interact around safety. But I also need to understand what the critical risks are in my work function and how I ensure that I engage my team in controlling those risks."

One thing Kenan and his colleagues have demonstrated time and again is dedication to the positive safety principle of 'be curious'. In 2022, Unitywater repeated the earlier organisational culture and safety maturity surveys.

"On Sentis's safety maturity model, we've moved from counterproductive up to public compliance. But if you look at the data set, in which there are over 21 elements, there are many of them already in private compliance, and there are some at the collaboration level. Four elements that were in counterproductive have jumped two levels up to private compliance."

These surveys provided other insights that catalysed new initiatives. *"We've been at this for five years, and we've reset things all the way through. I think that you have to always be willing to reconsider your approach."*

One significant realisation was that usage of their primary risk control tool was sitting at only about 40%. Bringing people in to tell them what they felt about it, they were told that it was too bureaucratic and cumbersome. *"You're on to question eight or nine before you even have anything about the actual risks."* This insight led to a reassessment and simplification of the process, including software improvements.

A second insight led to an initiative to enrol *"our whole leadership group into their [individual] roles as safety leaders for their systems... That's how we moved from a business with four or five safety professionals who were expected to be the ones keeping everyone safe, to 80 leaders all being accountable for safety."*

What this has allowed the safety team to do is invest less time in policing and more time on making improvements.

"Most of our work in the safety function now is running assurance on our systems and our safety management practices. And we always find gaps. You're always going to find stuff when you've got a business that's got all the complexity and risks that ours has. The key is to be just ahead of the game, find issues early and deal with them."

There are two other factors that have played a significant part in Unitywater's journey towards positive safety: clear communication and the solid support of the company's board.

Communication came early – with a lot of attention given to listening.

"When we got that data, we were able to debrief in a way that brought people into the conversation about what we were trying to achieve, and how they could play a role in that. Did it make sense? Was it the right thing? It became almost like an ongoing consultation process…

"What also started was a mechanism by which we could gather feedback on an ongoing and sustained basis around the way that people experienced the organisation. We captured all the feedback, every single session that everyone went through. And it wasn't just feedback about our Shape program and how they experienced that. It was about the organisation and the way that they interacted with each other and how they felt about their interactions with the business.

"We started to change stuff like toolbox sessions and pre-starts. We have a 'start and finish on site' approach at Unitywater. [We used to think] it was more efficient that [technicians would take a car home and then] go directly to the job next morning. But what we picked up from ongoing dialogue and collaboration with our people was that actually we missed important opportunities at the start of the day to set certain expectations, to see how people were feeling, to make sure that people were switched on to certain things.

"So we're working on actually going back to starting at the depot. The 30 minutes that we might lose on travel [wasn't worth it]. So little things like continuously picking up feedback, using data to complement that feedback cycle, and now we're looking at what's in the next iteration."

Kenan is grateful for the support for safety that has come from Unitywater's board.

"Boards in general need to be switched on to the importance of safety, and ensure they're not just ticking the box around their obligations and safety management system. That is only going to get you so far. You need to understand the context of your organisational culture and whether that is an impediment or an enabler for your safety outcomes. And then they need to be really inquisitive over what is actually going on. [In order to achieve that], they need to support management with the allocation of resources to actually find out what's really going on. Then those insights that come from that can help them to shape a much sharper program. But if you're a board member, you need to look at a causal model, not just whether we are compliant with ISO."

Over time, the board's focus shifted from TRIFR to more expansive metadata analysis that could reveal much more about what was really going on.

"Boards are being compelled to look beyond physical safety and safety management systems; psychosocial risks and the code of practice are actually going to drive this even further. Psychosocial risk, work design, work overload; those things are now part of our risk assessment and there's a positive duty [to be on top of those]."

"Our board recognised that this shift was necessary, and they were reassured in their directors' obligations and duties by the safety improvement they were seeing. If [safety performance] had been going backwards, it may have been more challenging to make this shift."

Kenan sees plenty of opportunities ahead on the Unitywater safety journey. *"We're nowhere near the finished product yet. We've still got a long way to go."* But all the work is paying off. In the financial year 22/23, Unitywater had their lowest ever TRIFR and lowest ever rate of LTIs – all without focusing on those measures.

"We've found that the reporting rates are really good now; people's willingness to flag stuff is really good. Overall, it's a much more constructive and healthy place to be than what it was when we first started this journey."

A FINAL WORD

We opened the book by asking the question, "How serious are we about safety?" and looking at examples of contrasting safety cultures. In the cases of OceanGate and the Fukushima Daiichi Nuclear Power Plant, safety was assumed to be everywhere, but it proved to be nowhere. Safety was 'committed' to. It was visible. But the underlying safety cultures were negative, with protection of life and property always lagging behind expedience and profitability. The actual commitment to safety in these cases was only skin deep, and both organisations paid a terrible price.

The contrasting example was the Tōhoku Electric Power Company, which through its preparations for and response to the Fukushima earthquake demonstrated a genuine and positive commitment to safety. Tōhoku's leadership had the courage to walk the walk on safety, not just talk the talk.

Unfortunately, as research by us and others has demonstrated, a majority of companies – in Australia and around the world and across many industries – still operate with traditional safety cultures that are highly reliant on compliance and that focus almost entirely on physical safety. This has led to a situation in which rates of physical harm have plateaued and rates of psychosocial harm are increasing.

All too often, workers' experience of safety is that their leaders demand compliance with safety protocols without demonstrating any genuine belief in a positive safety experience. Workers don't feel valued and supported. They do not feel engaged, motivated, or empowered when it comes to looking after their own wellbeing or that of their colleagues.

Positive safety takes a quite different approach, one that not only improves safety outcomes across the board but has beneficial ripple effects that go far beyond physical safety. Organisations that are able to create and sustain a positive safety culture – and we have shared a few good examples in this book – are doing so through their safety leadership, with the robust support of senior leadership and their boards. These leaders are taking a holistic, three-dimensional approach to safety that integrates the physical, social, and psychological experiences of the workplace, nurturing a culture within their teams and the wider organisation in which people can thrive.

Positive safety means moving well past the assumption that simple compliance with safety protocols will be enough to achieve zero harm. It means understanding the role of the human brain in response to safety; understanding about how your people are thinking and feeling – their attitudes – and how their behaviours follow. It means understanding the sources of your people's motivations and the ways in which their physical, social, and psychological experiences affect these.

We have described eight principles of positive safety and, in a very practical sense through the experiences of a number of our clients, we have demonstrated how these eight principles can be applied across different circumstances and contexts.

A significant common theme amongst all these organisations has been the genuine dedication to a positive safety culture at every level of leadership, from the board to the frontline leader. Success has come from walking the talk, from appreciation of the brain's role in attitudes and motivations, and from ongoing dedication to taking the journey towards a mature safety culture.

Safety citizenship is the goal, characterised by care and collaboration, shared responsibility between management and staff, and a holistic view in which safety is defined in terms of the three dimensions of the safety experience: social belonging and psychological health, in addition to physical wellbeing.

Shifting away from the traditional way of doing safety and towards a positive safety approach does require change. It may challenge your organisation and its leadership to shift priorities, to collect different data, to hire or promote different people. It will certainly require a focus on a different definition of safety. But we can tell you with absolute certainty that it's worth the effort. Because at the end of all of this, it's not just about improving your safety statistics. It's about driving a positive experience of safety that brings out the very best in your people and your organisation.

LIST OF RESOURCES

Scan the QR code to our Positive Safety Community portal and gain free access to the following useful resources.

Sentis Community Portal:

- The *Positive Safety Community* portal. Connect with safety leaders and specialists all over the world in an engaging community of peers, and access free and paid learning and resources to enable you to thrive in your safety leadership role.

Case Study:

- *Major Utilities Company Discovers an Opportunity for Improved Serious Incident Focus (2023)*. Sentis was engaged in 2019 by Unitywater, a major water utility company in Queensland, to understand the causes of SIFp (serious injury or fatality potential) events and improve the management of Unitywater's high-risk activities and safety culture. Our experts analysed over 650+ incidents and near misses, as well as over 1,000 hazards using our Meta Incident Analysis® (MIA) analysis methodology, and the learnings and recommendations as a result of this analytical process are captured in this report.

Reports:

- *Unpacking Safety Experiences: Employee Perceptions of Safety Climate (2024)*. This report analyses responses from a sample of 29,390 who participated in the Sentis Safety Climate Survey, to look through the lens of physical, psychological and social experiences of safety and gain an understanding of where organisations should be focusing their attention to move forward in building a strong, positive safety culture.

- *The State of Safety Culture in Mining – Industry Report (2022).* Featuring data from more than 21,539 mining workers across coal, metal ore and non-metallic minerals, this special edition industry report takes a closer look into what's working well and the biggest opportunity areas for the sector and how this compares to the broader cross-industry benchmark for safety culture performance.

- *The State of Safety Culture in Utilities – Industry Report (2021).* This report features data from more than 6,889 utilities workers across electricity and gas, infrastructure and maintenance, network and supply, renewable energy, waste management, and water and sewerage. This special edition industry report takes a closer look into what's working well and the biggest opportunity areas for the sector and how this compares to the broader cross-industry benchmark for safety culture performance.

- *Driving a Positive Safety Culture (2020).* Drawing insights from more than 21,711 workers across industry, we've summarised the key recommendations from our report into one handy checklist for leaders.

- *Underreporting of Safety Incidents in the Workplace (2018).* This report combines quantitative and qualitative data to uncover patterns in underreporting as well as the three key reasons why people underreport. It examines details and responses from employees across the agriculture, construction, education, government, industrial services, manufacturing, mining, oil and gas, and utilities industries.

- *The State of Safety Leadership (2017).* When it comes to driving a positive safety culture and safety performance excellence, it's hard to deny that strong, effective leadership is crucial. Yet, only 24% of leaders demonstrate strong safety leadership behaviours, according to our latest study of 8,747 employees across heavy industry. For organisations whose leaders fall into the remaining 76%, poor or average safety leadership performance could be detrimental to safety outcomes.

Self-Assessments:

- *The Safety Climate Self-Assessment.* Our Safety Climate Self-Assessment is here to help you uncover where you think your organisation stands. By taking this brief quiz, you'll gain valuable insights into your perception of your organisation's safety climate, pinpoint areas that need attention, and identify strengths you can leverage to enhance workplace safety.

- *Safety Culture Self-Reflection.* While not a replacement for a formal diagnostic, assessing seven subsets of safety culture across the environment, practices, person, and leadership dimensions of our safety culture self-reflection tool can help you personally reflect on the safety culture of your organisation.

- *Psychosocial Safety Checklist.* This free reflective tool outlines the components of a psychologically safe workplace and the actions you can take to achieve one in your own organisation. Celebrate and 'tick' your strengths, while also considering where areas of opportunity may lie.

- *Positive Safety Checklist.* Positive safety is a flexible approach that seeks to provide a practical, evidence-based set of principles to help organisations identify their strengths, improve their operations and, in turn, improve their safety culture. Based on more than 20 years of applied experience, the positive safety checklist is designed to guide discussions, planning, and organisational change, using the eight positive safety principles.

- *A Roadmap for Change: Setting your Cultural Transformation Project Up For Success.* Discover key steps to consider before kicking off your safety culture improvement process. Once you have taken the time to review the roadmap, we encourage you to reflect on how you can put into place a personal action plan to support you on your safety culture journey. Consider the key action items you can implement within the next seven days and in the spaces provided, describe the actions that you can start, stop, or continue to facilitate change.

- *How to Have Supportive Conversations.* This toolkit is available to assist you in preparing for a supportive conversation with a member of your team. The downloadable toolkit includes a supportive conversation factsheet, preparation worksheet and a conversation prompt card. This toolkit can also be supplemented with additional resources found on the Sentis YouTube channel.

White Paper:
- *Critical Control Assurance white paper (2022).* There's a strong case to suggest that failure and ineffectiveness of critical controls, alongside deep-seated safety culture issues like underreporting play a role in the continuance of serious injuries and fatalities in the workplace. But what does this all mean, and where do businesses start to make a positive change to ensure more workers return home safe, each and every day? In this white paper, we explore the concept of critical control assurance and the role it plays in driving positive safety outcomes.

Sentis Webinars and Animations:
- *Sentis YouTube channel.* Learn about the neuroscience of safety with the Sentis brain animation series and access our webinar playlist.

AUTHOR BIOS

Dr Vanessa Cook

Vanessa Cook is a Doctor of Psychology, specialising in safety leadership and culture development, and has been providing coaching, training and consulting for over 15 years. In her seven years with Sentis, she has applied her expertise in workplace engagement and psychological safety, safety motivation and behaviour change, and positive psychology principles to design, develop and facilitate impactful training all around the world.

In her role as Head of Positive Safety, Vanessa dedicates herself to delivering practical, neuroscience-backed training and consulting to enable organisations to level up their leadership capability and safety culture performance. Her passion for enhancing safety is demonstrated by her unwavering commitment to empowering individuals to revolutionise their thinking. Vanessa works with leaders from all industries to implement a positive safety approach, driving meaningful change and creating the ideal conditions for both their people and organisations to thrive.

Anthony Gibbs

As the visionary CEO of Sentis, Anthony Gibbs spearheads the organisation's transformative mission to enhance the lives of individuals and organisations each day. Anthony embarked on his career in psychology within the complex addiction and clinical areas, later applying his expertise in interpersonal dynamics and behaviour change to the intricate landscape of organisational settings. During his impactful 15-year tenure at Sentis, Anthony has cultivated robust relationships and partnerships with organisations worldwide, helping them to understand safety drivers within their workplace, and crafting strategies to improve safety, wellbeing, and overall organisational performance outcomes.

Bringing a unique understanding of varied industries including mining, utilities, oil and gas, construction, healthcare, and retail, Anthony has skilfully steered the dedicated Sentis team who play a pivotal role in delivering exceptional safety outcomes for the organisations they serve. Through mentorship and educational outreach, Gibbs constantly strives to elevate and empower others. At the core of Anthony's leadership philosophy is a commitment to positive safety – a conviction that leaders who genuinely care about their people and their experience of safety will drive behaviours beyond compliance, ultimately leading to increased commitment, care and effort.

www.ingramcontent.com/pod-product-compliance
Lightning Source LLC
Chambersburg PA
CBHW050805270326
41926CB00025B/4547